RIGHT MY COLLEGE APPLICATION ESSAY

Christine Gacharná

Copyright © 2023 Christine Gacharna
All rights reserved
First Edition

PAGE PUBLISHING
Conneaut Lake, PA

First originally published by Page Publishing 2023

ISBN 979-8-88654-132-8 (pbk)
ISBN 979-8-88654-133-5 (digital)

Printed in the United States of America

This workbook is dedicated to all of my inspirations:

To Jonathan and Lexi, my first students, and all the interesting and colorful Gen Zers who use my instruction to tell their stories. Getting to know these students gives me incredible faith and optimism in the future of our world.

A big shout-out to all my hardworking adult students in Louisiana, especially those of you who left comments in end-of-course surveys that encouraged me or illuminated places where I could improve. If it hadn't been for y'all, I never would have pushed myself to create any of this. (SWIDT???)

To Dr. Wawa Ngenge, who deliberately disrupted my interview to teach me valuable lifelong lessons in classroom management resilience; to Sunny Ryerson and Dr. Barbara Holloway, who mentored me with integrity and kindness; and to Lee Melancon, who modeled leadership, enthusiasm, possibility, brilliance, and excellence. As my boss, he handed me two valuable gifts while we worked together at UOPX: (1) a memorable and motivating compliment and (2) the missing piece of the puzzle I was struggling to put my finger on that made all of this instruction come together.

CONTENTS

WELCOME
  Testimonials ix
  Preface xv
  How to Use This Workbook xix
  Understanding Academic Integrity and Copyright xxiii

COMMUNICATE
  Prewriting 3
  The "Five Whys" 7
  Overcoming Mental Models 14
  The 80/20 Rule of Righting 16
  The Steps in the Righting Process 20
  The Five Most Common Mistakes Students Make 25
  Noncognitive Variables* 28
  Thesis Statement 39
  Student Essay: Show Me, Don't Tell Me 43
  High School You Is Ending 45
  You Don't Sit Down to Write a Rough Draft 47

NAVIGATE
  Review: Rhetorical Modes and Organizational Methods 53
  Review: Topic vs. Thesis 55
  Rhetorical Modes and Organizational Methods 60
  Fifty Percent of Your Work Happens Here 63
  Research 67
  Outline 70
  Review: Five-Point "Hamburger" Essay Outline 72
  Narration + Chronological Outline 74
  Rough Draft 76
  Review: Putting It All Together to Tell Your Story 78
  Revising 79

PUNCTUATE
    Editing 85
    Final Draft 90
    Word Count 91
    Feedback vs. Criticism vs. Editing 92

BONUS
    The Blank Page 97
    Facing the Blank Page 100
    Writing Is a Complicated Art 103
    Mistakes No. 6–11 106
    The Twelfth Most Common Mistake Students Make 108
    A Note on Introductions and Conclusions 110
    Student Essay: Short Answer 114
    Student Essay: Short Answer 116
    Student Essay: Show Me, Don't Tell Me 117
    Student Essay: Lessons from Failure 119
    Student Essay: Significant Experience 121
    Student Essay: Unusual Way to Have Fun 123
    Student Essay: Research 124
    Student Essay: Research | Diversity 125

Index 129

WELCOME

TESTIMONIALS

"I wanted to let you know that last night I was admitted into the University of Washington!!! I want to thank you for everything you did to help me reach my goal. I ended up getting into every school I applied to! Thanks again,"—Tim R, Student

"Thank you for all the help with Tim's essays. He was so proud of the end result and we couldn't have gotten there without you. I so appreciate it."—Teresa R, Parent

"I highly recommend using Christine's expertise to help your child write his/her college essays. Christine provided assistance to my daughter when she was writing her personal essay for her application to the University of Oregon. Christine made personal connections with Darian to make her feel safe and know that her work and ideas mattered. Christine provided strategies that Darian could use in all types of writing. Most importantly, she gave Darian specific feedback on all aspects of the essay. Through the revision and editing process, Darian was able to improve her essay and still keep her voice present throughout it all."—Jodi B, Parent

"So, I was one of those students who put all of her eggs into one basket. I knew I wanted to go to the UO, & it was the only school I applied to. I didn't realize it at the time, but my entire college application essay was built on a "phrasal verb." I had no idea what that even meant but by the end of the process, I was confident that at least I was using a phrasal verb correctly. :) I also made one of the biggest mistakes most students make. I'm super grateful that I got that corrected before I hit 'submit.' Go Ducks! :)"—Darian B, Student

"ESSAY CURE strengthens a critical part of the college application—the essay! Her fun, easy-to-follow approach helps students relax, stay focused and create an essay that will express their strengths and uniqueness. Parents can breathe a sigh of relief knowing Christine has their backs! Thank you so much!"—Marnie B, Parent

"Christine is very supportive and she genuinely wants you to be satisfied with your essay. She is super proactive when it comes to editing/composing and gives advice that I still remember today when writing. The biggest thing I gained was how to approach an essay and the attitude when tackling a prompt, which is something I struggled with before. Christine answered questions really thoroughly, even giving examples that made writing easier. I would recommend ESSAY CURE to anyone applying to college or looking to improve their writing skills. She really wanted me to feel confident about writing and her advice always seemed to be focused on quality writing. In the end, I got into my top choice, U.S. Air Force Academy!"—Nathan P, Student

"Christine's experience with college admission essays is highly extensive. She helped me write a very strong essay from scratch that helped me receive admission to the University of Washington, as well as multiple other Universities. My writing skills overall improved throughout the process and I feel much more confident in my ability to write papers for college classes in the future. I highly recommend her book to any high school student applying to college."—Camden R, Student

"My essay is now so much better than when we first started. At first, I really didn't know what to incorporate into my essay; some things l went too far into detail on and some things I needed to elaborate more on. Showing me the places in my essay where I needed to "show" more than "tell" definitely helped me the most. Also, adding comments on my punctuation helped so much as I struggle a bit when it comes to that!"—Helen S, Student

"I'm super happy to inform you that I ended up getting accepted! I honestly have never had the sort of support that I received from you, and it was amazing. I'm beyond thankful for the opportunity and for all your help. Thank you so much!"—Angelina H, Student

"This was super helpful! I sent my essay to Mrs. Gacharna and the feedback was extremely constructive and helpful. And I got an A! Thank you, ESSAY CURE!!!!"—Kyle H, Undergraduate Student

"Thank you, Christine! I've been admitted to all the colleges I've heard back from so far: Georgia Tech, Cornell, Clemson with $20K/year in merit, UVA, Wesleyan College with $15K/year in merit, and WashU. ESSAY CURE helped make the college process much less stressful.

Going into my senior year, I didn't know what I wanted to write about, and I felt a lot of pressure around the Common App essay in particular because colleges kept emphasizing how important it was for admission, and the prompts were really lofty. The most I had done with essay writing was the five paragraph "AP Lit" essay, and I quickly found that that approach wasn't going to cut it for my college essay. It was hard to decide what to write about because I'd read a bunch of examples of college essays online (like "Examples of College Essays that Worked") and I didn't know how I would even go about writing an essay like that.

You made the process so much easier by helping me brainstorm and write an essay that made my application more personal to me. It even turned out that my Common App essay was one of the strongest parts of my application. Showing you ideas for drafts and running drafts by you was enormously helpful for me because it gave me an honest, expert opinion from someone with a lot of insight into the perspective of college admissions officers.

RIGHT MY COLLEGE APPLICATION ESSAY

The most helpful part for me was the process we went through. First, I would show you a draft. If it was on the right track, you would point out directions I could take it or encourage me to do some more thinking and get back to you. I went through a lot of drafts, but even though this sounds like a lot of work, I was actually felt very relaxed and on-target about it.

Overall, ESSAY CURE definitely made the college process a lot easier and less stressful to navigate. I would definitely recommend ESSAY CURE to a friend and I know ESSAY CURE would be super helpful to parents who are stressed about college stuff coming up next year."—Elizabeth B, Student

"I was accepted into Virginia Tech and I will be attending this upcoming fall!! I am super excited and it was my first choice. Thank you SO MUCH for all of your help."—Rachel S, Student

"I think it was a valuable experience for all of us, and I hope that Libby has recognized the amount of effort needed to write a good essay or paper. We spent quite a bit of time discussing how to effectively communicate important ideas and maintain author's voice with limited word count requirements. Very hard to do well. Thank you for all your help, advice, ideas and guidance—we could not have done this without you!!"—Alyssa E, Parent

"My writing skills improved throughout the process in almost all areas. I couldn't have done any of this without you! Thank you!"—Camden S, Student

"Thank you for helping me write my college essays. I have just been accepted into UVA and am very grateful for all that you have done to make me a better writer."—Jonathan M, Student

"Hello, Christine. I just wanted to thank you for your work with Marin, particularly yesterday. As you well know, this personal statement & essay is pretty intimidating to these kids, and it's easy to see why. You really helped illuminate a lot of things to her and I feel like she has a new sense of peace, focus & confidence about it all. Because she's Marin, she did a deep dive into NU's page (not for the first time) and is pretty motivated about their dual-track that results in a BS in Engineering and a BA in Communications. It just seems like such a great fit for a young lady with a clear aptitude for STEM, but also possessing tremendous soft skills (she already has more environmental/emotional awareness than 90% of the adults I've ever met; she hears what's not being said and can take the temperature of a room/situation very well). It was also fantastic specific advice when it came to the potential benefit of being a young lady applying for an engineering department at a school like that. She was pretty energized last night (though probably not nearly as much as I was!) and I just wanted you to know that your time and skillful help were greatly appreciated on this end. Cheers,"—Jay C, Parent

"I just got some really good news this afternoon that I was accepted into the CalTech fly in program! I just wanted to thank you again for helping me out with those essays, I'm sure they boosted my application a lot. Thank you!"—Jimmy M, Student

"I got into UVA!!! I am so thankful for all of the help you gave me in writing my Common App essay and preparing me to write my other supplements. Also, just all of the college help you gave me in general was so useful. I am very sure that my essay was one of the reasons I was able to get in. I am so relieved to have gotten through this process with the success I wanted and I am so thankful that you helped me through it. Thank you so much!—Emily W, Student

"If I had not told you before, I made it into VCU! I started my first class this Tuesday and things are going fine. Currently, I am on the course for studying a pre-nursing major. I was surprised by how much I could change my essay and make it better in my end result. When I thought that my essays were finished and solid, there was always something I could change and make better. I would recommend this course to my peers. Thank you for your support! God bless :)"—Samantha M, Student

"I just heard back from UVA, and I got accepted early decision! Thank you so much for all the help you gave me, it definitely helped. As I did early decision, I'm done applying to colleges. Thanks again for all your help."—Nolan H, Student

"Hi Christine!!! I got into UVA!! I am so excited to be attending there next fall and this couldn't have been achieved without your help! Thank you so much for everything and my family will definitely be contacting you when my younger brother starts the application process! Go hoos! 💙🧡"—Paige C, Student

"Christine did an outstanding job working with our son. She was insightful and quickly helped him shape a great essay for several universities. Christine was thorough and responsive throughout the entire application process. I am confident that her help was instrumental in his successful acceptance at the University of Virginia. ESSAY CURE has my highest recommendation!"—Damion H, Parent

"Christine helped our son become a better writer by providing the tools and techniques to write effective papers or essays. Her program is highly organized and the content and her instructional style kept my son engaged throughout the process. In particular, Christine was always available to meet with my son to support the planning and development of his college essays and we were pleased that he was accepted to almost all of his college choices. We had such a great experience that we plan to have our daughter work with Christine to help with her college essay process."—Will C, Parent

"Christine with ESSAY CURE is truly amazing! I would highly recommend ESSAY CURE to any family with a student heading off to college. Christine is available, punctual and flexible. She really helps her students to think on their own so their unique individuality is represented in their essay. My daughter took the class and without hesitation we will be signing up again when her brother is ready. She is now off to Virginia Tech. We couldn't be more proud! This class is a must, you will not be disappointed! Thank you, Christine!"—Molly W, Parent

"Christine went above and beyond to help our son Joey without much notice. Her wisdom and experience with the college application process was much appreciated. However, it was her ability to review and provide feedback on his college essay and answers to specific questions on the applications was invaluable. Christine is an excellent writer and editor of others thoughts and words. I highly recommend Christine's services to everyone out there who has kids that are getting ready to apply to colleges."—Molly A, Parent

"Hello Christine, I also just wanted to say thank you so much for all the time and effort you put in to helping me reach the point I'm at right now. I wouldn't have been able to do it without you."—Tyler W, Student

"FIRST ACCEPTANCE! Hi there!! Just wanted to give you an update and let you know I got accepted into VCU's Pre-Medical Lab Science Major 😁."—Sofia H

"Christine at ESSAY CURE was amazing support and guidance. Christine worked closely with our daughter to find her voice in the writing. As we know, each college doesn't have the same essay requirements and Christine was able to take the framework and help with the different nuances as they applied to various schools. The results were amazing. She got into every college she applied to, ultimately choosing Clemson. We are counting down to moving day. We are thankful!"—Heather M, Parent

"Hi Christine! Kayla just got accepted!!! We are so grateful for all the help you gave her. I'd love to write a review or do anything that I can do to say thanks. This is literally her dream come true."—Kim G, Parent

"GUESS WHO JUST GOT INTO NOTRE DAME! Thank you thank you thank you for everything, I couldn't have done it without you"—Carolyn H, Student

PREFACE

My ah-ha moment came as I was working with a dozen or so high school seniors on their college application essays.

Well, wait. Let's back up a bit.

At the time, I was an associate faculty member at the University of Phoenix (UOPX) teaching undergraduate COMM and English courses.

What I saw was students white-knuckling their way through a rough draft, concentrating most of their efforts on the mechanics of *writing* (grammar, spelling, and punctuation) without understanding the *academics* of *academic writing*.

Falling back onto the familiar muscle memory of "writing a rough draft" that got them through high school was not working for them at the undergraduate level—especially not at the UOPX. See, the thing about UOPX is that there are no Scantrons for exams; almost every assessment in every class is an academic essay.

When I would pull students aside, they could give me the answers to the questions I asked based on course readings and instruction, and this frustrated me. I knew they were completing the readings and assignments and I could see that they were learning and yet their knowledge wasn't being properly measured in their grades.

As I paid more attention, I noticed that "testing" students via an academic essay brought up the muscle memory of frustration in the self-proclaimed "bad writers" and bad habits in the self-proclaimed "good writers." I began to notice that students identified with these labels that had likely been assigned long before and affirmed in high school.

My students could learn the material presented to undergraduates. They knew how to write. They simply didn't have a solid foundation in *academic writing*.

Academic writing is any writing that fulfills a requirement for an assignment to convey ideas in ways that are descriptive, analytical, persuasive, or critical.

Its purpose is to:

1) demonstrate the writer's understanding and synthesis of material and
2) aid the reader while communicating complex concepts and ideas.

Academic writing needn't be intimidating. Students are grateful and super relieved to learn that academic writing is not a draw-from-the-depths-of-your-soul effort.

Academic writing follows formulas.

Like learning how to drive, fly an airplane, or use a camera in manual mode, academic writing is a technical skill. Like all technical skills expertly taught, academic writing can be learned and, with practice, eventually mastered.

*****

There's no better way to master an art than to teach it, and that's what happened to me as I was untangling this dilemma in my teaching job. I retraced my own learning of English, Spanish, and journalism. I audited courses, and I poured over student essays from business, criminal justice, and nursing disciplines to identify patterns and common mistakes.

Then I rolled up my sleeves and got to work *developing an effective way to teach the fundamentals of academic writing* to help my dedicated students. I wanted to arm students with the tools for the job so they could get out of their own way and focus instead on the complex concepts and ideas they were learning in all of their classes. I wanted undergraduates campus-wide to be able to demonstrate understanding and synthesis of learning in the essays they wrote, and to earn good grades.

I showed my students the steps in the writing process and how professional writers let that tool do the work.

I created the Steps in the Righting Process to guide students as they worked their way through a process that had seemed nebulous and arbitrary before.

I introduced the Pareto Principle, and once I got buy-in from that, I showed them the 80/20 Rule of Righting that I created to help them measure their work.

I watched as faces lit up with relief when I'd tell them they didn't have to draw from the depths of their soul to write the great American novel, and I noticed the discomfort in faces who were now being challenged to abandon innate talent that had worked quite well for them up to this point. These students were and remain my most challenging students. Those I've been able to reach demonstrate tremendous growth, promise, and polish of truly the great writers and communicators that our world needs.

I do not believe writing is a "soft skill." I believe writing is a technical skill that serves as an essential component in an interconnected and global economy as any professional who does not master confidence in communication suffers greatly as a result.

Academic writing follows formulas. The steps in the writing process are the foundation for applying those formulas and, when used with the Steps in the Righting Process and the 80/20 Rule of Righting, the writing becomes the easy part.

My students were successful—so successful, in fact, that it wasn't long before my leadership recognized their progress. I was promoted to Lead Faculty for Communications and was responsible for spearheading policy and efforts to streamline the evaluation and assessment of student writing across campus. With all instructors using this method for grading student writing, our campus began to model as a team the cross-curriculum writing instruction that produces successful communicators.

Interestingly and surprisingly, I found it quite easy to get my campus peers on board with this instruction and evaluation. I attribute this largely to relief, as many instructors, especially STEM instructors, had very little patience with complicated rubrics for grading student work. My 80/20 Rule of RIGHTING freed them from the resentment of having to double as "English teachers" and sent them back to being the content expert teaching their students new and complex concepts and ideas.

*****

Voilà. Meanwhile, I had two high schoolers at home: a senior and a junior on track to graduate early, plus my friends' kids and my kids' friends. Eventually, it dawned on all of them that they had a college writing instructor in their midst, and before I knew it, I was knee-deep in reading college application essays.

Just like with my university students, I immediately saw the patterns, students clearly not using the steps in the writing process and unable to guide or measure their own progress. How could I tell? Well, the essays would begin and end at "rough draft," for starters, gave no consideration to the reader, showed limited to no organization, and most were written using the wrong rhetorical mode and organizational method, both tenets of academic writing at the undergraduate level.

And that's when I had my *ah-ha* moment.

In 2017, I created *essaypalooza!* to share my time and talents as a successful college writing instructor with high school students looking to land acceptance letters from colleges and universities. I wanted to be sure that once they got in, they were armed with the knowledge of how to succeed in academic writing at the undergraduate writing—because *college*.

In 2019, I started approaching high school administrators to get in front of high school juniors *before* they started writing their college application essays. What I was told time and again was *wow, this is great, and it's great what you're doing for high school seniors and all, but what you're talking about here is higher-level curriculum development and what we'd really like is to get you in front of our sixth graders before they take their SOLs.*

Then 2020 happened and during lockdown, I expanded as *ESSAY CURE* to help students of all grade levels from all backgrounds to understand the framework for academic writing that grows and develops with the student from elementary to middle to high school to undergraduate courses and into their adult lives. My goal is to create a solid foundation for effective communication, because while not all undergraduates are English majors, all college graduates write. Students do not need to be innately "good writers" to learn how to effectively communicate within their discipline—they simply need the instruction for confidence and encouragement to continue the practice. When students receive this consistently, across the board, their skills as an educated communicator improve and polish.

Communicate. Navigate. Punctuate. is the trademark of my writing instruction. I used the highly technical skill of teaching student pilots how to fly as my inspiration and model to transform the vague and nebulous idea of writing into the practice of a tremendously useful technical skill. I designed this workbook for motivated students who want a self-study approach to this instruction.

Welcome! I'm so happy you are here.—Christine Gacharná

THE STEPS IN THE righting ~~WRITING~~ PROCESS

01 RHETORICAL MODE & ORGANIZATIONAL METHOD

Chronological
Spatial
Progressive

Expository
Descriptive
Persuasive
Narrative

02 PREWRITING

free-writing

clustering
brainstorming
listing
5WH$

03 RESEARCH

04 THESIS

topic = subject, thesis = premise
A thesis is the writer's point of view gleaned from info & research. The thesis is what the writer has to say about the topic. A statement or theory that is put forward by the writer as a premise to be maintained or proved.

A thesis should be easily stated in 25 words or less.

05 OUTLINE

06 ROUGH DRAFT

07 REVISING

08 EDITING

09 FINAL DRAFT

© 2020 Christine Gacharna All Rights Reserved

HOW TO USE THIS WORKBOOK

Writing is not a wholly linear process. Writing is a complicated art, and even though this workbook focuses on "academic writing," it's still writing.

Stay with me here.

This workbook was written from a big-picture, top-down perspective. If you are a bottom-up learner or a highly detailed person, you may notice that the "Steps in the Righting Process" are presented out of order. This is by design. In fact, I spent a year in Photoshop and four more years tweaking the ins and outs of this one graphic until I felt it properly illustrated all of the main concepts I work so hard to instill in my students:

- It's not about the *writing*! Academic writing is about the *thinking* and the *doing* of academic learning.
- Fifty percent of the work is done in the first two steps—and I'm handing you half of it!
- You don't "sit down to write" a rough draft.
- Students who write what later becomes a noteworthy lede have no idea of their own brilliance during the freewriting stage. That's the whole beauty and point of freewriting.
- Don't tell me about your passion; show me what your interests led you to *do*.

And last but not least:

- "How's my content?"

While the "Steps in the Righting Process" follow the same principles and ideas as the steps in the writing process that all professional writers use (present company included,) they highlight for students the components of writing that I lovingly refer to as "invisible writing." Invisible writing stems predominantly from rhetorical modes and organizational methods, both tenets of academic writing at the undergraduate level. Most students won't study these nuances of writing in-depth until college, and that's the catch-22—first, they have to get in!

Parents often come to me and say, "My student is a really good writer," or students come to me with their shameful secret as the last resort: "I'm not a good writer."

My answer to both is the same.

It. Doesn't. Matter.

Academic writing is a technical skill. Technical skills, like photography, yoga, or flying airplanes, are learned; with practice, technical skills are eventually mastered. The "Steps in the RIGHTING Process" are designed for students to learn this technical skill, beginning with their college application essay so that they might eventually apply it as an undergraduate to write a compare-and-contrast essay in Econ 201 or a research essay in Bio 201 to earn good grades and be successful in their academic pursuits.

Like all technical skills, it's one thing to learn something conceptually and intellectually, but it's another thing entirely to actually be able to perform it (and then it's next-level to teach it, fun fact). The "Steps in the RIGHTING Process" are presented out of order in this workbook to force students out of their comfort zone of "sitting down to write a rough draft" and instead show them how to physically orchestrate the invisible writing work of the *thinking* and the *doing* that is academic writing because the rough draft is actually created by working through the steps in the process.

Like unlearning a bad golf swing, it's the "good writers" who prove to be my biggest challenge in this work, as it takes persistence and a lot of work to convince these students to relax their standards of perfection and relearn the technique from a different mindset. Freewriting is designed to be approached with the reckless abandon needed to truly brain dump their ideas onto the page with a total disregard for mechanics. The greatest college application essays I've seen were born from a single sentence mined from a freewriting exercise.

Asking someone like me to "edit" your writing is a bit like brushing your teeth while you're eating!

If you really want to take advantage of my expertise, you'll come to me and ask instead, "How's my content?"

The "Steps in the RIGHTING Process" are presented out of order in this workbook (with "The 80/20 Rule of RIGHTING" overlayed on top) to force students to do the *thinking* and the *doing* of working toward focusing on what it is they're trying to say, getting the biggest benefit of return from the work they put in on their freewriting exercises. The linear process of the steps is not nearly as important as the nonlinear process of transposing thoughts onto the page. Students can use "the five whys" to help procure a freewriting winner and to identify the answer to the question posed by the prompt (a.k.a thesis.) Students then plug the freewriting content into the outline that is built by the prompt, assignment, or invisible writing that you may not even be aware of yet that I'm about to hand you.

Bottom line: Don't get hung up on the order of the steps in the process. Simply follow along with the instruction. In my experience, the students who are willing to do the work to mine for the diamonds in the rough are rewarded with the gifts of their own brilliance.

Some of you will want to go rogue and skip around and do things out of order, and *usually*, I would tell you to rock on, but in this case, each step builds on the previous, so you really need to complete the work sequentially as I've presented it in this workbook for the best results. Some students choose to read through the entire workbook the first time and then come back to do the work. I can support that if you actually come back to do the work.

RIGHT MY COLLEGE APPLICATION ESSAY

In terms of how long it might take, that's up to you and your schedule. You could binge read the entire workbook and complete the steps one by one in a single day if you like that kind of intensity. Or you can set a goal for yourself to complete one step per day or one chapter per week. Whatever works for you.

The most important thing is that you read and act on each step and you save yourself enough time at the end of the process, so that you can go back and look at your essays objectively before the deadline for submission.

You're about to get really busy really fast as a high school senior, so my recommendation is that you start getting serious about working through the process somewhere around the Fourth of July and complete as much work on your college application essays as possible before Labor Day. This gives you plenty of time for final polishing before submission.

In a post-COVID world where many colleges and universities are making SAT and ACT scores optional, the essay may very well be the big differentiator. A lot is riding on this essay, not the least of which is landing acceptance letters with potential merit scholarships.

Welcome. I am honored that you're here and I look forward to helping you RIGHT your college application essay.

UNDERSTANDING ACADEMIC INTEGRITY AND COPYRIGHT

Okay, so even though this probably goes without saying, it's a good time to talk about *academic integrity*.

In a nutshell, what it means is colleges and universities can and sometimes will expel you for submitting work that is not your own. The temptation is real; so are the consequences.

Don't steal other people's work and try to pass it off as your own.

Oh, and there's this: colleges and universities have plagiarism checkers where student writing is submitted and scanned across a database of student work. Perhaps you've seen this? Perhaps you've even used it as a student at your high school?

Well, fun fact: these plagiarism checkers at the student level have only a fraction of the features they have at the faculty level. So don't think for a moment that just because this essay got submitted to MIT by your friend a couple of years ago that admissions officers at, say, Cal Poly or Virginia Tech, won't notice it's not original when you try to pass it off.

The college application essays in this workbook are used with permission from the student writers, and I've copyright protected this workbook; violating copyright infringements is a costly infraction.

My recommendation: avoid cutting corners. Just sit down and knock out the work.

Note to parents: Just as it's a rite of passage to parenthood that we step on a Lego in the dead of night and are routinely deprived the sleep we so desperately need, it's also an initiation ritual to endure the hours, expense, efforts, and logistics of preparing for college. This includes but is not limited to scheduling and paying for standardized tests, keeping track of deadlines, hovering over students to make sure they're getting things done, and paying attention to proper rest and nutrition. The adults who stand behind college applicants, the ones who break into a cold sweat whenever the letters F-A-F-S-A appear strung together in that order, are to be congratulated for their tireless efforts.

These parents are (understandably) extremely proud of their students whose hard work and resulting success will undoubtedly pay off in dividends.

The 2019 college admissions bribery scandal focused the spotlight on parents who rob their children of the opportunity to grow into healthy, functioning adults. Don't bribe your kid into college. Likewise, don't write this essay for your child. Don't send your child the message that you don't have much confidence in his or her or their abilities.

And then there's this: it's easy for those with a trained eye to identify which essays were written by a 40-something. (Two spaces in between sentences is a dead giveaway.)

Instead, encourage your student to work, study, prepare, write, and slog their way through the maze of frustration, anxiety, and sometimes despair that is the college application process.

The techniques in this workbook are proven to produce sound college application essays, but they won't work unless your student does.

Students are encouraged not to share their writing with you as they work through the process. The reason for this is that when the student has produced a solid rough draft, I want them to be able to glean an authentic reaction from you as their first reader. If you'd been watching the progression all along, it's harder for you to see the final product as a stand-alone work.

Communicate

01   **RHETORICAL MODE & ORGANIZATIONAL METHOD**

02 PREWRITING

03 RESEARCH   **04 THESIS**   **05 OUTLINE**

06 ROUGH DRAFT   **07 REVISING**

08 EDITING   **09 FINAL DRAFT**

02 PREWRITING

PREWRITING

> It is a tremendous act of violence to begin anything. I am not able to begin. I simply skip what should be the beginning.
>
> —Rainer Maria Rilke

It's no wonder most students skip this step. It's hard. It's work.

Academic writing writes itself by following the steps in the process. While thinking and doing are crucial elements to developing a successful essay, it's the thinking and the doing of this step, prewriting, that equals the remarkable digging in the dirt that ultimately produces a gem.

So while other students talk about "writing a rough draft" of their college application essay, just smile and nod. And then roll up your sleeves and get to work freewriting.

Prewriting is a tool to transfer ideas and abstract thoughts into words, phrases, and sentences on paper.

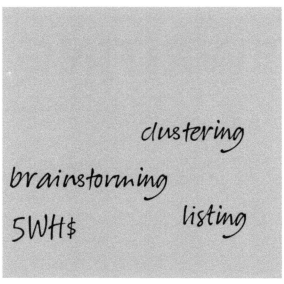

Prewriting techniques include clustering, brainstorming, listing, and the "five Ws."

There are numerous prewriting techniques, including freewriting, outlining, brainstorming, idea-mapping, and what's called the "five Ws." In this workbook, I focus on freewriting because our end goal is an essay and this is the fastest, easiest way to get words on the page.

Freewriting is the antidote to The Blank Page.

Freewriting is the name of a prewriting strategy used by writers to write loosely about any topic for a set amount of time (usually ten to fifteen minutes).

Before you groan, here's the good news about this step (actually, there's lots of good news):

- Nobody will see this but you;
- you don't have to worry about grammar,
- or punctuation,
- or spelling,
- or organization;
- it's not graded;
- it's not your final draft;
- you're not married to it; and
- you have nothing to lose but fifteen minutes.

RIGHT MY COLLEGE APPLICATION ESSAY

Freewriting is designed to help you get your thoughts and ideas onto the page without judgment.

Q: What do I write about?
A: Reflect on a time when you questioned or challenged a belief or idea.
Q: Why do I have to write about that?
A: Because even if none of the schools you are applying to use the Common App, you will still end up with a thoughtful essay idea on a topic of your own choice.

Choose an environment where you can focus, uninterrupted, for at least fifteen minutes.

Grab a pen or pencil and a blank piece of paper or open a new document on your device.

Set your smartphone to airplane mode, so you won't be distracted by notifications and set a timer for fifteen minutes.

Start writing.

Write "Reflect on a time when you questioned or challenged a belief or idea" and then write anything and everything that comes into your brain around this topic.

Don't overthink this. Just write.

Keep writing. Don't pay attention to your handwriting, fonts, grammar, punctuation, or spelling.

Write as fast as you can during the furious thoughts and record the mundane nothings during the not-so-furious times. Don't worry about who might read it or how it might sound later. Say everything you have to say about this topic.

At some point, you will find yourself stuck, thinking, *I don't know what to write about.* When this happens, write, "I don't know what to write about." Don't let yourself give in that easily.

When the fifteen minutes are up, that's it. You're finished. Pack it up, put it aside, forget about it. Walk away and go do something else. Your work here is done.

For now. :)

You may find you need to repeat this exercise two or three times. Try not to do them all in one sitting. Experiment with different topics. Use the "jumpstarts" from the Bonus chapter if that helps or choose from one of the Common App questions.

It's always a good idea to try a second freewriting exercise session using a different topic. For example, "Recount a time when you faced a challenge, setback, or failure. How did it affect you, and what did you learn from the experience?" Use the same process outlined above.

Later, after at least a day or so has gone by, review what you have written.

Ask yourself:

- Am I interested in this topic?
- Will my audience be interested?
- Do I want to be remembered by admissions officers as the kid who wrote about [insert topic]?
- Am I able to incorporate a noncognitive variable into my essay with this topic?

- If so, am I comfortable sharing that experience?
- Are other students likely to write about this same thing?
- Can I answer the question posed by the prompt in a way that relates directly to this topic?

Meanwhile, you may move on to the next few chapters, but wait until you feel confident that you have a prewriting winner before you start work in Navigate.

Do. Not. Skip. This. Step. "I know this already" is an easy target for what Steven Pressfield calls The Resistance, especially in students who consider themselves "good writers."

Does Tiger Woods know how to hit a golf ball? Yes, he does. Yet we don't hear him saying, "Nah, I don't need to follow the protocol of a practice swing. I know this already."

Do. Not. Give. Up. "This won't work for me" is how The Resistance will target especially the students who consider themselves "bad writers."

In my experience, it's the students who love math and science who benefit the most from this process. There are no "bad writers" knocking out a college application essay. If you are a qualified candidate with the necessary credentials to attend college, then this will work for you.

No matter who you are or how The Resistance has chosen to mess with you, I recommend you wake up fifteen minutes early each day for a week and knock out this exercise. By the weekend, you'll have several different options to choose from. You might end up choosing one of them and repeating the exercise on that same topic, trying to squeeze more out of it.

The most effective, astonishing, original college applications I've seen have been written here in the prewriting trenches. Notice I said, "prewriting trenches." I didn't say "rough draft." Remember that.

Loosely put words to the page. This is the step where you're mining for the diamond in the rough.

THE "FIVE WHYS"

Once you're able to force yourself to comfortably freewrite for at least fifteen minutes, it's time to level up your practice and find your *why*.

The "Five Whys" is a technique used to explore cause-and-effect relationships that often identify an underlying problem by repeating the question, *Why?* Each answer forms the basis of the next question.

Oftentimes, students are not able to do this on their own. At Essay Cure, our coaches work extensively with students to do this difficult work.

If you want to give it a whirl and go at it alone, this is what we recommend:

Some students find it easier to record this practice on a device and transcribe it later, rather than to write it out. Other students benefit from asking a parent or a friend to "push" them through the questioning process. Try practicing the Five Whys several ways to find the technique that works best for you.

Pro tip: The benefit of using a recording device during this exercise is that you'll have a backup plan if you utter a brilliant sentence and then immediately forget what you just said.

This is how using the Five Whys worked for one student to generate her answers to the questions posed by the prompt:

> The lessons we take from obstacles we encounter can be fundamental to later success. Recount a time when you faced a challenge, setback, or failure. How did it affect you, and what did you learn from the experience? (500–650 words)

Asking "*Why?*" enough times during freewriting reveals the crux of what writers are trying to communicate. When this student told me she decided to get a job, I asked, "Why?" and she started to tell me some very interesting things. I asked her to do a freewriting exercise on it:

> In May, I realized that COVID was not going anywhere any time soon. It felt like with every day came the news of something else I had planned for the summer being canceled. I decided that instead of staying locked up at home, I would find a job. All of the reasons I had for not having a job had been swept away by the virus, so I thought "why not?". After several rejections, I ended up getting hired at a Chipotle-style restaurant with one of my best friends. I spent

almost 40 hours a week there, every week, for the entire summer. I picked up everything pretty quickly, and soon became very proud of how I was performing. In July, I was asked to be a manager and gladly accepted the offer. Since then, I have been leading multiple shifts a week alone and participating in weekly management meetings. These weekly IDS (Identify, Discuss, Solve) meetings have quickly become a highlight of my week. We go over sales, costs, and overall performance from the previous week and identify areas for improvement. We discuss various factors that could contribute to these issues, and our roles in them. Then, we decide on action items that we can implement over the next week, and along with that, each member of the management team is given their own to-do/goal for that week. I had never been exposed to real life problem solving like this before now, and I really fell in love with the process. Seeing how one small thing can contribute to our much larger goals as a store made me realize how this could apply to my own life as well. Small habits and changes can change as much, if not more, as huge goals for yourself can. Also, when running a shift by myself, I have been forced to work out problems without the safety net of another person to help me out. If something breaks, it is up to me to fix it. If a customer comes in complaining, it is up to me to salvage their experience. I have enjoyed this independence, and have really seen myself grow in confidence and communication skills.

Toward the end, her answer to the first half of the prompt is illuminated:

Q: The lessons we take from obstacles we encounter can be fundamental to later success.
A: "Small habits and changes can change as much, if not more, as huge goals for yourself can…
    If something breaks, it's up to me to fix it."

The second half of the prompt asks, "Recount a time when you faced a challenge, setback, or failure. How did it affect you, and what did you learn from the experience?"
I asked her to do a freewriting exercise and write about something breaking while she was managing the restaurant and how she used "Identify, Discuss, Solve" to fix it:

The first time I led a shift by myself, busy Friday night only three of us, drive thru and inside lines building up, feeling high pressure. hurrying around, trying to make every order quick as possible, keep customers satisfied. not staying organized, barely any communication among us, struggling to keep up. I asked a coworker to grab a new bag of sauce from the back, and when he had not returned for a while, I headed back to see what was taking so long. As we had been rushing one another and running around hastily, he dropped the gallon bag of sauce right into the fryer, causing an explosion of burning sauce and plastic all over the floors, walls, and equipment. I stared at the mess in front of us, I forced myself to step back and reevaluate. IDS. I realized I was projecting my feelings of pressure and rush on my coworkers. We had been making little mistakes all night and focusing too much on speed rather than our customers' experience and the quality of our work. As soon as there was a free moment, I pulled the three of us into a mini shift huddle. I apologized and we all identified where we should be doing better for the rest of the night. We set goals for ourselves and agreed to keep one another accountable. We wanted to slow down and engage with our customers, since we knew that would create a better experience for both us and the customers. Following that shift in attitude, the three of us were much more in sync, we did not make any mistakes in orders, and our times were about the same as before, but our customers left much more happy and satisfied. Because we reorganized ourselves, resolved to stick to our established plan, and put more attention to detail in, we improved greatly in a short time.

We closed quickly and efficiently that night because we all had a good idea of what needed to be done and who was supposed to do it. Even though I ended up spending another hour there alone draining our fryer and scrubbing every surface from the exploded bag, I was extremely pleased with our ability to decide on ways we could improve as a team and quickly turn around a night headed in the wrong direction.

She learned several things in the process, the first of which is that it pays to free yourself from the confines of perfection when freewriting. It's a very difficult practice for many students to adopt, especially those who have high expectations for themselves and are inexperienced at challenging muscle memory.

Don't get hung up on the *writing*. At this stage, I want you focused on the *thinking* and the *doing* of following the Steps in the RIGHTING Process. Simply sit down to write with reckless abandon, paying no attention to grammar, spelling, or punctuation. Transcribing your thoughts into words and *including all of the content that you wish to communicate* to your reader is more important at this stage than perfecting spelling or the flow of sentences.

We took her freewriting and plugged it into the formula:

NARRATION + CHRONOLOGICAL

LEDE	ALL OF A SUDDEN,
SET STORY	PRIOR TO,
SHOW STORY	MEANWHILE,
CLIMAX	IN THAT INSTANT,
SHOW CHANGE	SINCE THEN,
PERSONAL SIGNIFICANCE	THESE DAYS,
MECHANICS	USE POLISHED GRAMMAR, SPELLING, & PUNCTUATION THROUGHOUT THE ESSAY

And then she worked to connect the paragraphs and shore up her essay:

> As I turn the corner, I have no idea what's on the other side of that wall. I'm met with a horrible smell of burning, and I see every surface covered in sauce. My coworker stands frozen, mouth wide open in shock, eyes on the floor avoiding mine. Processing the mess before me, I wondered where the night had taken a turn for the worst. It was a busy Friday night, the first time I led a shift by myself as a manager, and I had a very specific idea in my head of how I wanted the night to go. The pressure I was placing on myself was quickly building. As we had been working hastily, a coworker dropped a gallon bag of sauce right into the fryer, causing an explosion of sauce and plastic to flood the floors, walls, and equipment. Processing this chaos, I used the training I'd learned in our management meetings to force myself to step back and reevaluate.
>
> Before summer, I had plans to go to Kenya on a mission trip and to spend time serving within my church. I feel most fulfilled when I am helping others, so when the pandemic hit, I felt restless locked up in my house. The best solution for me was to get a job, and I was hired at Costa Vida, where I spent almost 40 hours every week for the entire summer.
>
> My hard work and dedication paid off in July, when I was asked to be a manager. I was taught to apply IDS, or Identify-Discuss-Solve, to solve big picture problems for the store and everyday mid-shift issues. I soon found myself applying IDS to issues I faced in all areas of my life, not just at work.
>
> I learned about myself that I can easily take the temperature of a room and hear what is not being said. I realized that I had been projecting my stress of wanting this night to be perfect onto my coworkers, making them feel pressured and rushed. I had started off the night with high expectations for myself, but as my ideal shift very quickly crumbled, it was now up to me to salvage what was left of the night.
>
> At a free moment, I pulled my team aside, knowing I could apply IDS. I identified my external stress and apologized, then established areas where we could improve for that night. We discussed solutions, set goals, and agreed to support one another with accountability. I was able to establish a plan to solve our issue. Even though I spent another hour there alone draining our fryer and scrubbing every surface from the exploded bag, I was extremely pleased with this improvement. If I were to experience this all over again, I would not prevent the chaos and explosion, as I never would have received the opportunity to recognize my faults in the sequence of events. However, I would keep us all there to clean up the mess together to build leadership. Because of my Type A personality, I know that I cannot completely stop placing pressure on myself to perform well,

but I can be intentional in recognizing how I express my internal stress and how that is projected onto and perceived by others.

Along with this awareness, my experiences managing at work have allowed me to grow my confidence and assertiveness. Because I have been solving problems and making tough decisions on my own, I have experienced successes and failures. Previously, a fear of failure has prevented me from even beginning tasks. I believed that everything had to be perfect on my first attempt at it. Leading shifts, I have faced many failures and endured the subsequent consequences. These struggles allow me to identify my own weaknesses, then improve myself, with others' advice and my own objectives. (640 words)

Notice that she didn't "sit down to write a rough draft" but instead followed the steps in the process, and by doing so, her essay came together just as I promised her it would. When students are willing to challenge their muscle memory and practice this type of writing, the results are astonishingly good. This is only one of the countless examples. I've noticed that the self-proclaimed "good writers" have a much more difficult time with this. My theory is that the "bad writers" have less muscle memory to fight and nothing to lose by trusting me in this work. Regardless, the process doesn't work unless you do.

Some of you would consider this a college application essay, but to the trained eye, it's still a rough draft. When I pointed it out at this stage, she saw that she tends to write every sentence with an introductory clause, writing mostly compound-complex sentences. This is quite common, especially in students who have a logical, mathematical brain, and she was applying to an engineering program. There's nothing wrong with beginning each sentence with an introductory clause, but after a while, it can feel repetitive, lulling a reader to sleep. It's best to break these up with short, choppy sentences. There's also nothing wrong with writing compound-complex sentences. But when the entire essay is written this way, it gets cumbersome for the reader to wade through.

This is exactly what revising and editing is for, and it's a quick fix. To do this work any earlier than this stage is the equivalent of brushing your teeth while eating. It's pointless, destructive, and counterproductive to the task at hand.

This is how her essay looked after she turned some sentences into short, punchy, noun-verb constructions for effect, broke some of the compound sentences into two sentences, and polished her thoughts:

> I turn the corner, no idea what will be on the other side of that wall. I am immediately met with a horrible smell of burning, and I see every surface covered in sauce. My coworker stands frozen, mouth wide open in shock, eyes on the floor avoiding mine. Taking in the mess before me, I wondered where the night had taken a turn for the worst.
>
> It was a busy Friday night, the first time I led a shift by myself as a manager, and I had a very specific idea in my head of how I wanted the night to go. The

pressure I was placing on myself was quickly building. As we had been working hastily, a coworker dropped a gallon bag of sauce right into the fryer, causing an explosion of sauce and plastic to flood the floors, walls, and equipment. Processing this chaos, I forced myself to step back and reevaluate.

Before the summer, I had plans to go to Kenya on a mission trip and to spend time serving within my church. I feel most fulfilled when I am helping others, so when the pandemic hit, I felt restless locked up in my house. The best solution for me was to get a job, and I was hired at Costa Vida, where I spent almost 40 hours every week for the entire summer. My hard work and dedication paid off in July when I was asked to be a manager. I was taught to apply IDS, or Identify-Discuss-Solve, to solve big-picture problems for the store and everyday mid-shift issues. I soon found myself applying IDS to issues I faced in all areas of my life, not just at work.

I have found that I can easily take the temperature of a room and hear what is not being said. I realized that I had been projecting my stress of wanting this night to be perfect on my coworkers, making them feel pressured and rushed. I had started off the night with high expectations for myself, but as my ideal shift very quickly crumbled, it was now up to me to salvage what was left of the night. At a free moment, I pulled my team aside, knowing I could apply IDS. I identified my external stress and apologized, then established areas where we could improve for that night. We discussed solutions, set goals, and agreed to support one another with accountability. I was able to establish a plan to solve our issue. Even though I spent another hour there alone draining our fryer and scrubbing every surface from the exploded bag, I was extremely pleased with this improvement.

If I were to experience this all over again, I would not prevent the chaos and explosion, as I would never have received the opportunity to recognize my faults in the sequence of events. However, I would keep us all there to clean up the mess together to build leadership. Because of my Type A personality, I know that I cannot completely stop placing pressure on myself to perform well, but I can be intentional in recognizing how I express my internal stress and how that is projected onto and perceived by others.

Along with this awareness, my experiences managing at work have allowed me to grow my confidence and assertiveness. Because I have been solving problems and making tough decisions on my own, I have experienced successes and failures. Previously, a fear of failure has prevented me from even beginning tasks. I believed that everything had to be perfect on my first attempt at it. Leading shifts, I have faced many failures and endured the subsequent consequences. These struggles allow me to identify my own weaknesses, then improve myself, with others' advice and my own objectives. (632 words)

RIGHT MY COLLEGE APPLICATION ESSAY

This essay worked in seven of the eight noncognitive variables! That's incredibly difficult to do, but as she shows, it's not impossible. I also want to give kudos to her—students who show up and do the work, the hard work of the thinking and the doing, R<small>IGHT</small> the most successful essays.

She was offered a full-ride scholarship from one of her state universities and got into her reach school. :)

OVERCOMING MENTAL MODELS

Fold your arms. Go ahead, it's not a trick question.

Now unfold your arms and fold them again, this time with the opposite arm on top.

How does that feel?

Write down three words to describe it. This is important, we'll use these words later.

For thousands of years, people tried to run a four-minute mile. Nobody could.

Experts said for years that the human body was simply not capable of a four-minute mile. It wasn't just dangerous; it was impossible.

Then, in the 1940s, the mile record was pushed to 4:01. Runners struggled with the idea that, just maybe, the experts had it right. Perhaps the human body had reached its limit.

Mental models. We all have them. It can help us make sense of the world—and it can keep us stuck. Every mental model is really a short circuit to understanding reality but mental models developed over time through experience can make all of us resistant to instruction.

A mental model is simply a way we understand something.

A mental model is an explanation of someone's thought process about how something works in the real world. It is a representation of the surrounding world, the relationships between its various parts, and a person's intuitive perception about his or her own acts and their consequences. Mental models can help shape behavior and set an approach to solving problems (akin to a personal algorithm) and doing tasks.

Put another way, mental models are beliefs, ideas, images, and verbal descriptions that we consciously or unconsciously form from our experiences and, once formed, guide our thoughts and actions within narrow channels. These representations of perceived reality explain cause and effect to us and lead us to expect certain results, give meaning to events, and predispose us to behave in certain ways.

Although mental models provide internal stability in a world of continuous change, they also blind us to facts and ideas that challenge or defy our deeply held beliefs. They are, by their very nature, fuzzy and incomplete.

Some of the characteristics of mental models are:

- they are incomplete and constantly evolving;
- they are usually not accurate representations of a phenomenon as they typically contain errors and contradictions;
- they are stingy or frugal and provide simplified explanations of complex phenomena;

- they often contain measures of uncertainty about their validity that allow them to be used, even if incorrect; and
- they can be represented by sets of condition equals action rule.

Politics are a mental model. Each political view has a certain viewpoint on many topics and issues. But given the wide array of issues and views, each individual political viewpoint would surely have shortcomings—information that is missing or ignored. Without curiosity, how will students discern the difference between policies? (Hint: They won't because they can't. Therefore, it's important for students to show traits of curiosity.)

The same is true throughout our lives. Every mental model we have consists of both strengths and weaknesses. And we rarely examine why those models are there, or where they come from.

On May 6, 1954, Roger Bannister broke the four-minute barrier, running the distance in 3:59.4. The next year, another runner broke the four-minute mile barrier.

Today, well-trained high school athletes easily and routinely break a four-minute mile.

The college experience is all about examining and challenging mental models. Your success as an undergraduate and, later, as a college graduate will be determined by how well you allow yourself to be stretched.

Q: How do I recognize when my mental models are being challenged?
A: Remember your three adjectives from earlier that you used to describe how you felt when you folded your opposite arm on top? Those are the feelings that The Resistance will evoke.

Whenever those three adjectives arise while Righting your college application essay, pause for a moment to examine your thoughts. Recognize these adjectives for what they are—your mental models being challenged.

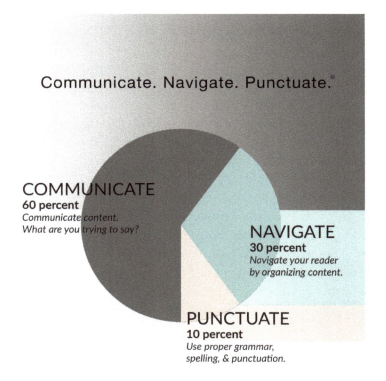

THE 80/20 RULE OF RIGHTING

The Pareto Principle (also known as The 80/20 Rule) is named after an Italian economist who observed that twenty percent of the population in Italy owned eighty percent of the land.

The Pareto Principle is an aphorism—a pithy observation—that states eighty percent of outcomes can be attributed to twenty percent of causes.

Put another way: Twenty percent of effort is going to account for eighty percent of results. Some examples of how the 80/20 Rule looks in everyday life:

- We wear twenty percent of our clothes eighty percent of the time.
- Twenty percent of the carpet in our home gets eighty percent of the wear.
- In business, twenty percent of customers make up eighty percent of income.
- Eighty percent of crimes are committed by twenty percent of the population.
- Eighty percent of all traffic accidents are caused by twenty percent of drivers.

Knowing this rule, we can start putting it to work for us in every area. For example, the next time you pack an overnight bag, grab the clean clothes from the top of the dryer. Those are the clothes you'll be looking for once you arrive at your destination. Then consider: what's the one event I'll be attending while I'm there? Pack the clothes you'll need for the event and Boom. Done.

The 80/20 Rule of Righting *is our twist on the Pareto Principle, adapted specifically to academic writing.* We call it *Communicate. Navigate. Punctuate.* It's the trademark of our instruction, and it works like this: *if you spend more time on the things that produce the biggest benefit of your results, guess what? You'll get better results.*

In the case of the college application essay, stop spending all of your time and energy focusing on grammar, spelling, and punctuation, and instead focus on freewriting exercises designed to get you to elaborate on; *what am I trying to say?*

This combats the first of the five most common mistakes students make when writing their college application essays. It seems that it would go without saying, but you'd be surprised. You *must* answer the question posed by the essay prompt, and you must do it in an engaging way that makes you jump off the page, separating you from those who look like you academically in other areas of the application.

I use the alliteration of *Communicate. Navigate. Punctuate.* to help you remember the 80/20 Rule of Righting as you work your way through the Steps in the Righting Process. These tools will serve you tremendously in academic writing at the undergraduate level, starting with your college application essay.

Academic writing is, first and foremost, an assessment of student writing. It's an assignment or an exam, and it will earn you a grade. As a student, it's your job to effectively communicate in order to demonstrate synthesis of learning. Academic writing uses an objective tone and simple, concise, predictable sentences and structure to demonstrate learning.

When we overlay the 80/20 Rule of RIGHTING onto the Steps in the RIGHTING Process, it looks like this:

Gray represents the Steps in the RIGHTING Process that focus on *content*. What are you trying to say? The answer to that question, the content you are trying to communicate, equals sixty percent of the work. If you don't know what you're trying to say, how will you write an essay that convinces an admission officer of that? What is your answer to the question the prompt is asking? Which story from your life experience appropriately and best illustrates this answer? *Communicate equals content.*

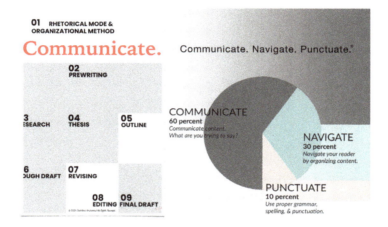

Blue represents the Steps in the RIGHTING Process that focus on *organization*. Academic writing follows predictable structure and organization to demonstrate learning. Navigate equals thirty percent of the work, so why are you spending sooooooo much time fretting over grammar, punctuation, and spelling when you don't even understand the organizational method or rhetorical mode? Don't worry. I'm going to hand it to you. *Navigate equals organization.*

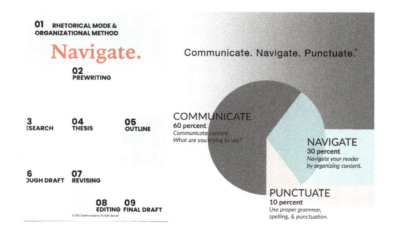

RIGHT MY COLLEGE APPLICATION ESSAY

Notice how little *pink* is sprinkled into the graphic? *Pink* represents the Steps in the Righting Process that focus on *mechanics* of grammar, spelling, and punctuation, and while important enough to be its own step in the process, it's the very last step. Fretting over mechanics while writing is like brushing your teeth while eating—totally counterproductive to either task. *Punctuate equals the mechanics of grammar, spelling, punctuation.*

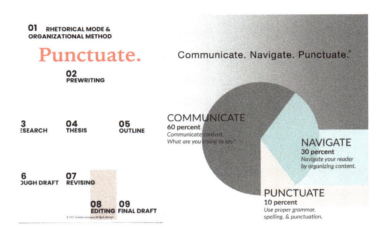

When I was teaching undergraduates, I discovered that many students don't understand the basic premise of academic writing, so we're going to start there by working backward from the answer key.

In my experience, students come to me and ask, "Will you edit this for me?" Students spend most of their time fretting over grammar, spelling, and punctuation when the question they really should be focused on is *How's my content*? and formulating their college application essay into a proper academic essay, using the correct rhetorical mode and organizational method.

Q: Whoa. Wait. WHAT?

A: Communicate. Navigate. Punctuate. is our 80/20 Rule of Righting and, paired with the Steps in the Righting Process, is the formula I'm going to hand you. In fact, I'm going to hand you the formula for every academic essay you write as an undergraduate. It's called "Rhetorical Mode and Organizational Method," and we'll get to that. But first, I want you to understand how to maximize your 80/20 Rule by using the Steps in the Righting Process.

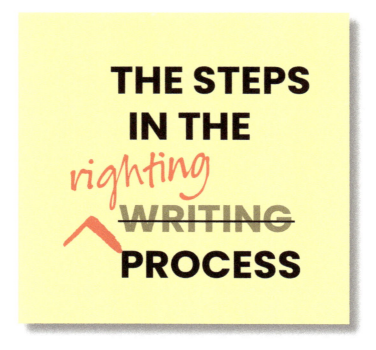

THE STEPS IN THE RIGHTING PROCESS

Imagine boarding an aircraft with a pilot who skips over the first five steps and ignores the last three steps of a pre-flight checklist! And then tell me how you'd feel about flying to, say, Shanghai with that person?

And I'll tell you that's exactly how I feel when I open an essay that begins and ends at "rough draft." I can spot it immediately. It opens with very little attention paid to me as the reader. There was no effort made to get me interested or make me curious to learn more. The writer is taking for granted that I'm going to continue reading—but what if I don't?

If your audience is an admissions officer, that person is under no obligation to keep reading if the essay isn't interesting or engaging. After all, there are likely tens of thousands more essays clamoring for their attention.

Writing doesn't happen in the "rough draft" stage—it develops as the writer works through the steps in the writing process.

As your instructor, I've adapted those steps here specifically for students looking to write academic essays. I've overlayed The 80/20 Rule of RIGHTING onto The Steps in the RIGHTING Process to give you a big-picture overview of both.

It looks like this:

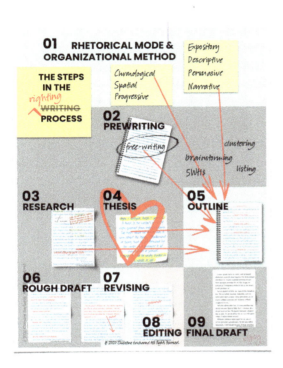 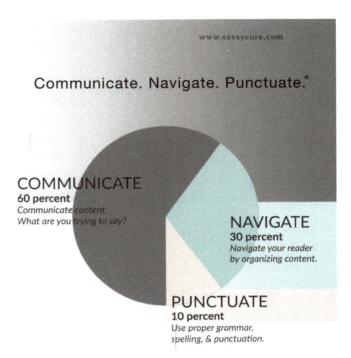

I know. It's a lot. Don't worry; each chapter and each step will serve to break this process down into bite-size chunks to help you realistically Right your college application essay, and they are the same steps you can use later for academic writing at the undergraduate level.

Notice the steps represented in blue? That blue indicates what I call "invisible writing." Without it, there's no clear direction of where things started or indication of where things might go, or what a reader might expect to glean from sticking around.

Invisible writing is to academic essays what the skeletal system is to the human form: it gives the essay predictable and polished structure, and academic writing is all about structure.

The technical term for this invisible writing is called "rhetorical modes and organizational methods." Rhetorical modes and organizational methods are the first step in academic writing, and if you're not fully aware of this step, chances are you've either been leaving it out, or you've been struggling to squeeze your college application essay into the wrong rhetorical mode (We'll explore this more in Navigate).

Notice the steps represented in gray? Those are the steps that focus you on the content of what you are trying to communicate.

I'd like to point out that fifty percent of the work on your college application essay is done in the first two steps! I'd also like to point out that the thesis statement, located in the heart of the page, comes before "rough draft."

Admissions officers can spot students who start and end at "rough draft" as soon as they open the essay.

That's what almost happened to Caroline.*

Like most students who consider themselves "good writers," Caroline didn't come to me asking for help with writing. She was convinced that she already knew how to do this.

In a Common App essay about "a talent that was so meaningful," her first sentence was:

"Caroline, you have a personality disorder."

Only, Caroline doesn't have a personality disorder. She was using the term for shock effect, but she wasn't recognizing how a reader with a different filter might see that sentence (perhaps a reader who really does have a personality disorder? Or a close family member who struggles with one?)

She went on to spend 363 of 604 words total praising the French horn player who encouraged her to join high school band. Only she didn't capitalize "French."

In another essay, this is what she wrote as a personal statement:

> *Penn State: Please tell us something about yourself, your experiences, or activities that you believe would reflect positively on your ability to succeed at Penn State. This is your opportunity to tell us something about yourself that is not already reflected in your application or academic records. We suggest a limit of 500 words or fewer.*
>
> I really don't want to tell you something about myself. I've already told you about marching band in the Common App essay. I'm extremely dedicated to band, so I could tell you more about that but I don't think that's what you want to hear. I know you want to hear a different side to me. I just don't know what to tell you about. I'm seventeen years old—my life experiences are very limited. I've been to magnificent places around the world. When in Colorado, my family and I went white water rafting. That's an entire story right there where I could talk about how I was scared but overcame my fear and went down the river and had the time of my life. I was thirteen, I don't know what the time of my life is. (443 words)

Hmmm.

In her defense, it wasn't entirely her fault. High school didn't really use the rhetorical mode that she needed for her college application essay, so she did what her muscle memory told her to do: she squeezed her thoughts into a five-point hamburger essay, awkwardly trying to create an introduction where none was needed.

And when she got frustrated with the process, she turned to sarcasm. We'll talk about sarcasm later, but the bottom line is that it's a low-level form of anger, and I don't recommend using it.

Caroline needed to RIGHT her college application essay.

She listened. She learned. She used the Steps in the RIGHTING Process and our 80/20 Rule of RIGHTING.

RIGHT MY COLLEGE APPLICATION ESSAY

Caroline's next essay invited her reader in and *showed* her answer to the question posed by the prompt. Not only did she push herself in the process, but she also mined a diamond in the rough in one of her freewriting exercises that remains one of my favorite ledes of all times:

It was fast and high: a combination for trouble.

She got in. Caroline was admitted to Penn State and UVA, among other schools.

Jimmy was looking to major in engineering, but English is not his first language. Jimmy was grateful to learn that he didn't have to draw from the depths of his soul to write the great American novel, but he was still nervous that this writing instruction wouldn't work for him.

He had to challenge his mental models and the muscle memory he'd developed in writing high school essays. Instead of "sitting down to write a rough draft" as a self-proclaimed "bad writer," he had to force himself to do the prewriting exercises that he considered silly.

I pushed him. I put him on the spot and asked him questions, taking him through the five layers of why and taking notes of his answers. He got more and more uncomfortable with answering the question, *Why?* Jimmy learned that he could trust me as he watched his document evolve and improve as we worked through the steps. He saw his work from prewriting take shape on the page.

He learned to ask me, "How's my content?" rather than asking me if I would "edit" his essay for him.

As you struggle with the freewriting exercises, I want you to think of Jimmy because as you're trying to decide whether or not I know what I'm talking about, Jimmy is unpacking his bags in his dorm room at CalTech. The acceptance rate at CalTech is *six percent*. Jimmy gave me permission to share his essay with you, and I will, in "Student Essay: Show Me, Don't Tell Me."

Emily got into UVA. So did Adam, Nolan, Paige, Jonathan M, and Libby. Jonathan G and Marin got into Northwestern. Nathan got into the US Air Force Academy. Tim and Angelina and Cameron got into UW. Elizabeth L got into Oregon State and, like many of our students, earned herself a sizeable academic scholarship to help pay for it.

We show academically qualified students how to RIGHT a college application essay that separates them from those who look like them on paper, and we do it using the same techniques used in college essay writing, because—*college*! What if you get in?

By my calculations as a former college English and writing instructor, you'll write ninety-two pages of essay your freshman year. You can't afford the time it will take you to sit and stare at the blank page.

My whole mission here is to challenge your mental models and retrain your muscle memory to approach academic writing from a new direction. Instead of "sitting down to write a rough draft" as you did in high school, I want to show you how to RIGHT an academic essay as an undergraduate. I want you to choose your rhetorical mode and organizational method to knock out the first thirty percent of your essay before you even get started on the content you'll plug into your essay. I want you to figure out what you're trying to say (generating content and determining a thesis), solidify your outline, and stop fretting about grammar, spelling, and punctuation. Seriously. Forget about grammar, spelling, and punctuation for a while. We're not concerned with that (yet).

I'm going to push you out of your comfort zone, and that's okay because you've already identified what that feels like for you. You've learned how to recognize that uncomfortable feeling, and hopefully, I've convinced you that feeling is nothing more than stretching you in ways that your muscle memory doesn't want you to go. We all know that our muscles were made to be stretched and pushed to failure to strengthen and grow.

Because—college. Lots of students are valedictorians, have 34s on their ACTs, and 4.0-whatevers on their transcripts, and they're all competing with you for seats in the freshman class.

First, you must get in.

How do you separate yourself from those who look like you academically on paper? By Righting a college application essay that makes you jump off the page. In this post-COVID 19 era where colleges and universities are increasingly making standardized tests optional, the weight the college application essay carries in your application has never been more critical.

Up next: Common mistakes and noncognitive variables. Before we get started on the Righting, I want to get you started on choosing your topic. Let's examine some of the common mistakes students make, how not to make them, and look at qualities in a student that admissions officers might be looking for that perhaps you haven't considered.

*Not her real name

THE FIVE MOST COMMON MISTAKES STUDENTS MAKE

Working backward from the answer key, let's first examine the five most common mistakes in a college application essay:

1. *Beginning and ending with "rough draft."*

    The reason we talk so much about muscle memory in this workbook is that high school students tend to "sit down and write a rough draft."
    And then they bring me that draft and ask, "Will you edit this for me?"
    As you work through our workbook, you'll begin to see how this is such a dead giveaway at the undergraduate level for students who do not understand academic writing.
    Notice how many steps in the writing process a student ignores by starting at rough draft to write a college application essay:

    - choosing the correct rhetorical mode and organizational method,
    - prewriting exercises designed to identify a topic that exemplifies the student's character and personality,
    - identifying a succinct one-sentence answer to the question posed in the prompt and communicating this answer with clarity and purpose,
    - demonstrating efforts to learn about the school to which the student is applying, and
    - polishing the presentation to consider the reader.

    Writing a purposeful essay requires following the sequential steps in the writing process—and since academic writing is a technical skill, it's not about the writing per se, but rather the *thinking* and the *doing*. Since the thinking and the doing happens during the steps in the process, essays are written by completing those steps!
    In this workbook, we'll work on retraining muscle memory, so that students come to us long before they reach the "rough draft" stage and ask instead, "How's my content?"
    We do this because if the content is "meh," we don't want you wasting your time creating an ineffective rough draft.

2. *Preoccupation with mechanics.*

Mechanics, albeit important, are the main consideration in the final steps of the process (editing). Fretting about grammar, spelling, and/or punctuation in the early stages equals not using time and attention efficiently.

It's kind of like brushing your teeth before you eat dessert.

Remember the 80/20 Rule of Righting? Eighty percent of outcomes can be attributed to twenty percent of causes.

Put another way: twenty percent of effort will account for eighty percent of results.

Therefore, if you spend more time on the things that produce the biggest benefit of your results, guess what? You'll get better results.

Knowing this, students should pour all their energy and efforts into focusing on:

- What is my answer to the question the prompt is asking?
- Which story can I tell from my life experience that appropriately illustrates this answer?
- Why am I spending sooooooo much time fretting over grammar, punctuation, and spelling when I don't even understand the organizational method or rhetorical mode and I haven't even looked at the essay prompt or determined what it is that I want to say?

Don't focus on mechanics until you reach the "editing" step in the process.

3. *Testimonials.*

A testimonial is a public tribute that testifies to someone's character.

Many students love, admire, and/or respect a particular family member, coach, teacher, or mentor who has positively affected them along the way.

Writing a touching testimony to, say, Couch Lou tells admissions officers about what a great person he is—and no doubt, most of them would agree. Coach Lou *is* great!

However, is that testimony going to answer the question of why you chose their university to apply to?

Couch Lou, being the stellar person he is, would almost certainly appreciate reading such a testimonial. I encourage you to consider writing it—only write it as a heartfelt note of gratitude and thanks (different rhetorical mode and organizational method). In the days leading up to high school graduation, this will make for a very meaningful gift to that special person. There's a lesson in the bonus chapter that shows students how to write a heartfelt thank-you that recipients will appreciate and cherish in four minutes or less. Please visit essaycure.com for free instructions on how to Right a 4-Sentence Thank you.

Meanwhile: limit Couch Lou's involvement in your application essay to the scope in which he participated in *your* story: how you turned to him for help and how his advice or help guided you to take the actions you did.

If you feel strongly about including a family member, coach, teacher, or mentor in your college application essay, review the chapter on "noncognitive variables" for more information about incorporating a strong support person in your essay.

4. *Answer. The. Question.*

I know. You'd think this would go without saying, but you'd be surprised.
It's called an "essay prompt" because the "prompt" is "prompting" you to write an essay about a certain topic or to answer a specific question—as clearly stated in the prompt.
Answer. The. Question.
Pro tip: Make sure you adhere to word count restrictions.

5. *Submitting inauthentic work and violating academic integrity.*

Asking parents to write the essay, purchasing an essay online, using an essay that worked for a friend—there are several reasons why this is a mistake, beginning with violations of student codes of conduct and academic integrity (easily detected by plagiarism software) and ending with parenting fails.
Ethical issues notwithstanding, it defeats the whole purpose of the college application essay: for the college to get to know you through the nuances expressed in your own unique voice and the experiences you choose to share in illustrating your interest in a particular academic program. Nobody can tell your story like you can.
At the very least, I can promise you: this isn't the admissions officer's first rodeo. But even if it is, it's easy after reading a few dozen essays or so to see which ones have the voice and wisdom of a forty-something. These people are reading tens of thousands of essays. They can tell.
And then there's this: what if you get in?
I show students how to write academic essays at the undergraduate level, and I start with the college application essay for exactly this reason. What if you get into your dream school? Do you imagine there may be some expectation of you to be able to handle writing a research paper in Bio or a compare-and-contrast essay in Econ?
I want my students to have the confidence and ability to be able to master academic writing at the undergraduate level. The college application essay is only one rhetorical mode, but the framework for using the Steps in the Righting Process and the 80/20 Rule of Righting will work for all academic essays at the undergraduate level.

NONCOGNITIVE VARIABLES*

Just as we do with writing the essay in this workbook, let's work backward from the answer key for a moment and look at the admissions process overall.

What are admissions officers looking for in a student?

In an article written by an education professor at the University of Maryland, College Park, and presented to the National Association of College Admission Counselors in Alexandria, Virginia, the key lies in quantifying "noncognitive variables."

Noncognitive variables were adopted to evaluate, admit, and retain nontraditional students on campuses nationwide. These variables have proven to correlate with student success in college *and* increase the diversity of a student population.

The research cited indicates that noncognitive measures predict the success of nontraditional students better than traditional measures of standardized tests and grades.

Researchers found if success is measured as retention or graduation, noncognitive variables have more validity than grades or test scores for both traditional and nontraditional students.

There are three basic ways a person may show ability:

Componential intelligence is the ability to interpret information hierarchically and taxonomically in a relatively unchanging context. This is an ability associated with a traditional experience in our society. If your situation was not relatively stable, or if your context was other than traditional, you are likely to have more trouble showing your ability in this way. Traditional admission measures that rely on standardized tests and prior grades rely heavily on this type of intelligence.

Experiential intelligence involves the ability to interpret information in changing contexts; to be creative. A person with nontraditional experiences may have had to develop and demonstrate this kind of intelligence to be successful.

The third type of intelligence is what RJ Sternberg in his book, *Beyond IQ*, calls *contextual*. This type has to do with the ability to understand and "work" the system to the student's advantage. For a person with a nontraditional background, it is critical to know how to interpret the system in terms that foster his or her development.

There is evidence that many different groups of students have nontraditional background experiences and can be more accurately assessed using noncognitive variables. The degree and form of nontraditional experiences vary considerably across groups, but with these and other groups, assessment using noncognitive variables can greatly facilitate admission decisions.

So what are these noncognitive variables, and how do colleges and universities go about assessing students within this framework?

The research presented is based on eight noncognitive variables defined as follows:

Positive self-concept or confidence: the student displays a strong self-feeling and writes about his or her strength of character, confidence, determination, and independence.

Realistic self-appraisal, especially academic. The student recognizes and accepts any deficiencies and works hard at self-development. The student recognizes the need to broaden his or her individuality.

Understands and deals with -isms. The student is a realist based upon personal experience of -ism. The student is committed to fighting to improve the existing systems. These students are not submissive to existing wrongs, nor are they hostile to society. Rather, they can handle -isms in our system. Ideally, the student asserts school or organization roles to fight -isms.

Prefers long-range goals to short-term or immediate needs. The student demonstrates the ability to defer gratification in favor of a long-range goal or plan.

Availability of strong support person to whom the student may turn in crises.

Successful leadership experience in any area pertinent to his or her background (church, sports, noneducational groups, etc.).

Demonstrated community service. The student is involved in his or her local or cultural community.

Knowledge acquired in a field. The student demonstrates knowledge outside of traditional classroom subjects. Unusual and/or culturally related ways of obtaining information and demonstrating knowledge are measured by noncognitive variables, especially if the field itself is nontraditional.

Broken down into more detail, here's how each noncognitive variable may look in both students who display and don't display these traits. While it's important to try to incorporate these traits where applicable in a college application essay, it's also important for students to recognize any unintentional messages that their essay may be communicating in the form of one of these variables. For example, students who do NOT display traits of noncognitive variables may be highlighting that information in the topics they choose to write about. It's worth studying both sides of each noncognitive variable in order to maximize the use of the positives yet also recognize the pitfalls of the negatives and then use that information to develop the content of the essay.

Positive Self-Concept or Confidence

Students who do NOT display this trait write about reasons why they might have to leave school, or are not sure they can make it to graduation. They write about other students being more capable, or how they expect to get marginal grades. They write about ways in which they will have trouble balancing personal and academic life. They avoid new challenges or situations, and this shows in their activities.

Students who display this trait write confidently about making it through college to graduation and make positive statements about themselves. They expect to do well in academic and nonacademic areas and assume they can handle new situations or challenges.

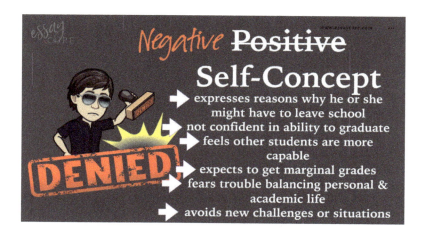

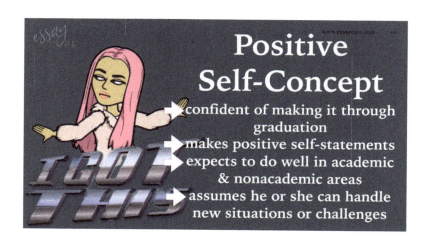

Realistic Self-Appraisal

Students who do NOT display this trait write about how they are not sure how evaluations are done in school. These students tend to overreact to the most recent reinforcement (positive and negative) rather than seeing it in a larger context, and their stories reflect this. They do not know how they are doing in classes until grades are posted. They do not have a good idea of how others, especially their peers, perceive them or would rate their performance.

Students who display this trait accept compliments graciously and write about ways in which their efforts are appreciated. These students accept rewards for achievement as well as consequences of poor performance. They understand that reinforcement is imperfect, and they don't overreact to feedback, be it positive or negative. They have developed a system of using such feedback to alter their behavior in a way that benefits them and helps them to grow.

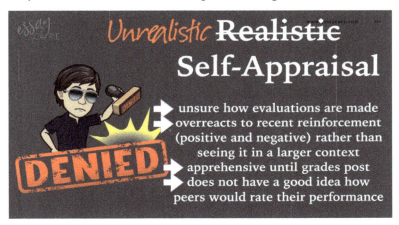

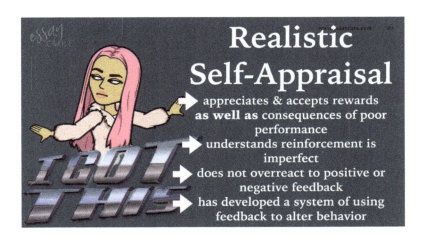

Understands and Deals with ~isms

Students who do NOT display this trait write about ways in which they are not sure how the "system" works. These essays center around either 1) a preoccupation with an ~ism or 2) about ~isms don't exist. They blame others for their problems, and they react with the same intensity to large and small issues concerned with ~isms. They do not have a successful method of handling ~isms that do not interfere with their personal and academic development.

Students who display this trait write about understanding the role of the "system" in their life and how it treats nontraditional persons, often unintentionally. They have developed a method of assessing the cultural/racial/gender demands of the system and respond accordingly: assertively, if the gain is worth it; passively, if the gain is small or the situation is ambiguous. They do not blame others for their problems or appear as a "Pollyanna" (excessively cheerful or optimistic) who does not see an ~ism that works against them.

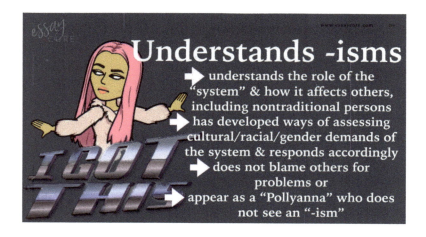

Prefers Long-Range Goals to Short-Term or Immediate Needs

Students who do NOT display this trait show little ability to set and accomplish goals and are likely to proceed without clear direction. This can show up as a byproduct in their essay. They rely on others to determine outcomes and live in the present. They do not have a plan for approaching a book, school in general, an activity, etc. Their goals tend to be vague and/or unrealistic.

Students who display this trait write about ways in which they can and have set goals. These students proceed for some time without reinforcement. They show patience and can see, identify, or write about the partial fulfillment of a longer-term goal. They are future and past-oriented and do not see simply immediate issues or problems. They show evidence of planning in academic and nonacademic areas.

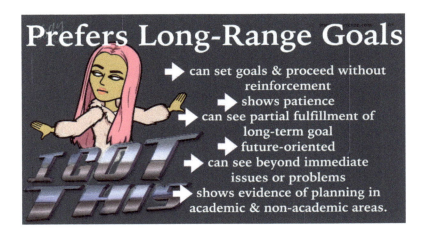

Availability of Strong Support Person

Students who do NOT display this trait do not show evidence in their essay of turning to others for help. Rather, they write essays about being a loner. They usually have no single support person, mentor, or close adviser, which may be apparent from letters of recommendation. They do not talk about their problems and/or they write about they can handle things on their own. Access to a previous support person may be reduced or eliminated as they relocate or enroll in a new school, and they are not aware of the importance of finding a new support person.

Students who display this trait write about having identified the need for and received help, support, and encouragement from one or more specific individuals. They do not rely solely on their own resources to solve problems. They are not loners and are willing to admit they need help when it is appropriate.

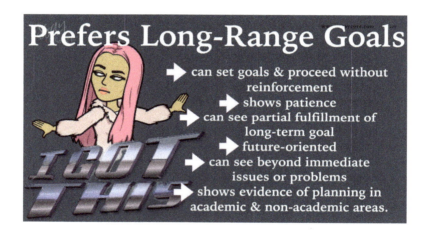

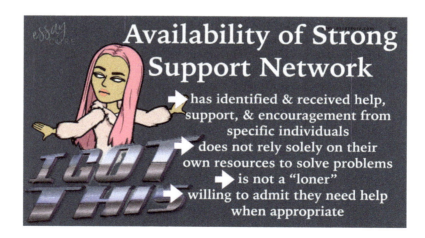

Successful Leadership Experience

Students who do NOT display this trait show no evidence in their essay that others have turned to them for advice or direction. They are nonassertive and do not take initiative. They are overly cautious and avoid controversy. They are not well-known by their peers.

Students who display this trait write about have shown evidence of influencing others in academic or nonacademic areas. They are comfortable providing advice and direction to others and have served as mediators in disputes or disagreements among their peers or even in their organizations. They are comfortable acting when and where it is called for.

Demonstrated Community Service

Students who do NOT display this trait tend to not be involved in a community. They have limited activities of any kind and are fringe members of any group to which they belong. They engage more in solitary rather than group activities (academic or nonacademic).

Students who display this trait write about ways in which the group they are identified with is cultural, racial, gender-based, geographic, etc. They have specific and long-term relationships in a community and have been active in community activities over time. They have accomplished specific goals in a community setting.

Knowledge Acquired in a Field

Students who do NOT display this trait appear to know little about fields or areas that they have not studied in school. They show no evidence of learning from community or nonacademic activities and are traditional in their approach to learning. They have not received credit-by-examination for books (AP or CLEP) and may not be aware of credit-by-examination possibilities.

Students who display this trait write about what they have learned or gleaned from a field or area that they have not formally studied in school. They have a nontraditional, possibly culturally, racially, or gender-based view of a field or profession. They have developed innovative ways to acquire information about a given subject or field.

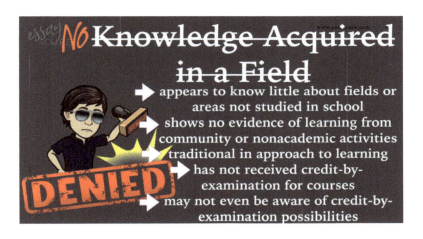

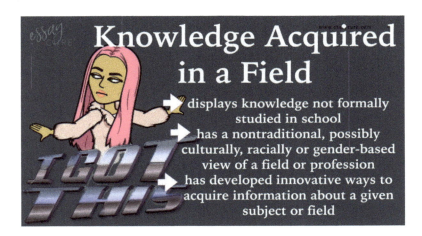

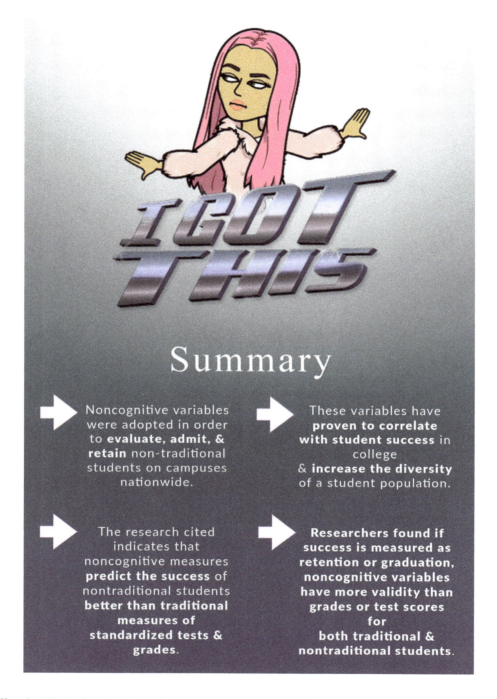

*Sedlacek, W. E. (1993). Employing noncognitive variables in admissions and retention in higher education. In Achieving diversity: Issues in the recruitment and retention of underrepresented racial/ethnic students in higher education. (Pp. 33–39). Alexandria VA: National Association of College Admission Counselors. Reprinted with permission.

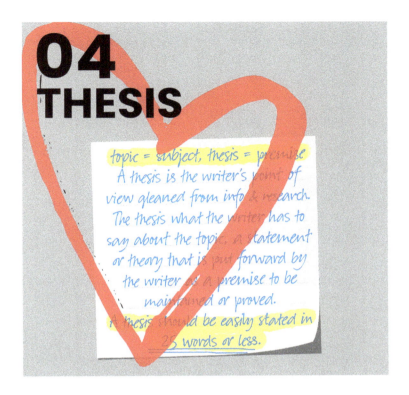

THESIS STATEMENT

Notice where we place *thesis* in the steps in the process?

It's no accident. The thesis statement is the heart of your essay.

It seems this would go without saying, but you'd be surprised: Make sure your one-sentence answer (which, in another rhetorical mode, would otherwise be known as the "thesis") actually answers the question the prompt is asking.

*In fact, this is T*HE *most common mistake students make when writing their college application essays: they don't answer the question posed by the essay prompt.*

I don't allow my students to make that mistake.

I insist my students paste the essay prompt to the top of the page while they are writing to keep the question top of mind. It serves as a visual reminder of the most basic tenet of college writing—answer the questions posed in the assignment. (Fun fact: I also insist students include either the Common App or the college or university the essay is for and word count restrictions for guidance and, later, efficiency.)

Most college application essay prompts will fit into one of these categories:

- Tell us something about you that we wouldn't otherwise know from your transcripts.
- Why us?
- A challenge to write a creative response.

Once you identify which category the prompt falls into, you can begin working on your one-sentence answer.

For example:

> In the MIT application, we're not looking for one long, highly-polished essay. Instead, interspersed throughout the application will be short answer questions designed to help us get to know you. Just be yourself.
>
> We know you lead a busy life, full of activities, many of which are required of you. Tell us about something you do for the pleasure of it. [100 words or fewer]

Easy.

This prompt falls into the "tell us something about you" category. It clarifies that the "something" needs to be something you enjoy, and it reminds you to write the essay casually, in your own words. "Just be yourself," it says.

Come up with a one-word answer on the topic of something you do just for the pleasure of doing. Then spend the next ninety-nine words supporting that one word—and remember, "just be yourself."

There's a reason that phrase was inserted into the prompt. Pay attention to the clues they are giving you! Don't try to be highbrow in your writing or choose a grandiose or exotic locale as a topic—unless, of course, you are an exotic teenager living in a grandiose locale who tends to speak with an air of highbrow. Be yourself.

Some prompts include compound-complex sentences. Some are poorly written. There's very little you as a student can do about that, and anyway, it doesn't even matter in the end because regardless of how poorly or how well the prompt is written, your process stays the same: follow the steps in the writing process.

Some prompts require you to answer more than one question in a single prompt.

For example:

"The lessons we take from failure can be fundamental to later success. Recount an incident or time when you experienced failure. How did it affect you, and what did you learn from the experience?"

In this prompt, the student must:

1. identify the incident and failure,
2. convey how this experience affected you, and
3. explain the lessons learned.

RIGHT MY COLLEGE APPLICATION ESSAY

This essay easily follows the narration rhetorical mode, chronological order, centered around the subject—the time when you experienced failure. The outline of this essay will separate each question from the prompt.

*****

So let's go back to the one-ish sentence answer to college application essay prompts.

To help you with this, visit essaycure.com for a preformatted Student Activity Sheet and guidance for best practices on filling it out. You will use this when submitting college applications and requesting letters of recommendation from teachers, and it will also help to remind you of all the things you've done that you might choose to write about.

While you're on our website, search for the "student strengths identifier." Many students find this homework for a parent or a trusted adult quite valuable in identifying topics or traits to write about.

Using these two resources, plus the freewriting you've already done, think about your life experience.

What defines you? What answers the question to the essay prompt?

Write that answer.

Hurry—write it quickly before your mind complicates it.

Some students benefit from dictating this answer into the voice memo of their smartphone and then transcribing it later.

Don't try to sound smart. Just jot it down (think "freewriting"). It should be a simple answer, one that you can say succinctly without explanation.

For example, write about a significant experience.

"I'm from a ranching family, but I don't like to ride horses."

That's a problem.

This problem became the topic of one of her essays and the solution she found to this problem became both her thesis and the story of her essay that she outlined, wrote, revised, and edited for the application to the college of her dreams.

"Cowgirl up," Gramps said.

That was her lede. She got in. :)

Another student wrote about how much he hated competitive swimming, avoiding it as a kid by convincing his parents to let him play the saxophone instead. Later, as a high school senior, he was forced as a lifeguard to swim a competitive race for the club's team. On the starting block next to him: the star swimmer from his school. No pressure.

Swimming was his topic. His story was about the difference between how lifeguards are trained to save (never dive into the pool. Never take your eyes off the struggling swimmer, tread water for hours, conserve energy) and how athletes train for endurance in competitive swimming (streamline dive, use physics to move through the water, swim as fast as possible.) The significance of what he learned was twofold: 1) that simply showing up can make all the difference and 2) as the leader responsible for these kids' safety, he now had an innate recognition of what to look for in a struggling swimmer.

His lede was:

I watched the 5 and 6-year-old freestyle swimmers closely as they splashed along to finish the 25-yard race.

He got in.

I'll share the actual essays with you in the bonus section, but I caution you not to read them until after you've done some freewriting exercises of your own.

Q: Why?
A: Because no one can tell your story the way you do. Almost every student feels The Resistance convincing them to doubt themself and doubt the process—until they watch it work and begin to take shape on the page.

It won't work for you unless you do the work.

I don't want you to get too caught up in examining how it worked for others; I want you doing the work of making it happen for yourself.

You've now learned two crucial steps in academic writing that incorporate so much information and effort—and we haven't even gotten to *rough draft* yet! Imagine sitting down to write a rough draft after learning all of this! Once you've seen it, it's impossible not to notice when it's missing.

In the case of the college application essay, skipping this step means making the first of the most common mistakes.

"Don't tell me the moon is shining;
show me the glint of light on broken glass."
—Anton Chekhov

STUDENT ESSAY: SHOW ME, DON'T TELL ME

There really is no such thing as a "safety school," as one student's "dream" can be another student's "probable." Unlike the SAT or ACT, where students across the country all face the exact same variables of questions and answers, Essay Cure students hail from all corners of the country, from diverse family backgrounds and incredible differences in life and educational experiences. There is no 1:1 comparison of our students. That's why the magic happens in the one-on-one coaching sessions, as each student is unique. We don't write these essays for students—we don't need to! Parents don't need to, either. Nobody can tell a student's story like a student can. The following essay was written by Jimmy, who was offered admission at CalTech, Cornell, and Harvey Mudd College. "Unfortunately, I wasn't offered admission to MIT, but I'm still really happy with the options I have," Jimmy said in an email.

Prompt: Think about an academic subject that inspires you. Describe how you have furthered this interest inside and/or outside of the classroom. (400-word limit)

"Wait. I thought I was supposed to fit the problem to the formula, not the other way arou—*a-ha*!"

It was the beginning of my ninth-grade year. I had signed up for an extra online math course with a site called Art of Problem Solving. I had always felt very proficient in mathematics, receiving top scores on every math test in middle school. I felt nearly invincible. To my surprise, Art of Problem Solving was a harsh reality check.

It was *hard*. Long gone were the days of plugging and chugging numbers into a given formula. Not a chance. Instead, we had to prove every single formula we wanted to use. The homework no longer resembled the lecture to a T, and I spent hours at a time just working on a single problem.

I asked for guidance from an instructor for the problem I was struggling with. Rather than telling me how to solve it, he suggested, "See if you can find a way to make Vieta's Formulas fit the question you are trying to solve."

That's when I found it. I realized if I just squared the formula itself, the pieces fit right into place. That single breakthrough was more satisfying than any of my top test scores. Why? Because I didn't just use the fact that $p+q = -b/a$ and $pq = c/a$, but I understood the foundations and made the formula my own. This way of learning shaped my passion for a deep understanding of math and engineering.

This unwavering curiosity has fueled all aspects of my academic pursuits. I want to dive deep and discover why. Why does Newton's Law of Cooling work? I wonder how he managed to figure that out. Can I really use $T(t) = T_s + (T_0 - T_s)e^{-kt}$ to uncover the timeline of a crime scene based on the temperature of a body? I can often be found discussing proofs of moment of inertia calculations with my physics teacher, or examining the complexities of integrating high-order partial fractions with my calculus teacher. Nothing surpasses the immense satisfaction I get from using my newfound rotational physics knowledge to calculate the individual torques required for our three-jointed robot arm, or grasping combinatorics enough to assess the probability of being seated with a friend during a seat change. (387 words)

IF YOU WANT SOMETHING YOU'VE NEVER HAD

You must do something
you've never done.

HIGH SCHOOL YOU IS ENDING

The student who wrote the previous sample student essay started out just like you. Bogged down with work, activities, and AP classes, Jimmy didn't have a lot of time—certainly not time to waste. He doubted these silly prewriting exercises were going to work for him.

Until he found the diamond in the rough:

"I thought I was supposed to fit the problem to the formula, not the other way around."

As he explored that topic more in another freewriting exercise, he discovered it was pretty easy to generate the missing words that he needed to plug into his outline. They weren't perfect, but that's okay. He'd worry about that later.

He spent some time thinking about the prompt. He took my advice and wrote it on a sheet of paper so he could hang it on his bathroom mirror. He put it on the home screen on his smartphone. Everywhere he went, he was forced to be thinking about his one-sentence answer to this question:

Prompt: Think about an academic subject that inspires you. Describe how you have furthered this interest inside and/or outside of the classroom.

I didn't write that essay for him. Anyone who knows me knows I can't use $T(t) = T_s + (T_0 - T_s)e^{-kt}$ to uncover anything other than nothing, let alone the timeline of a crime scene.

The thing is, I didn't need to write it for him! Not only is he perfectly capable of writing this essay himself, but he also wrote it better than anyone else could!

This is the point in the process where High School You might have started—and ended—had you not made the conscious choice to follow The Steps in the RIGHTING Process to write your college application essay. Think about what you've learned and all of the work you've done to prepare for this essay. Without all that thinking and doing, your essay wouldn't be a competitive part of your application.

    You are no longer one of those students: the ones who begin and end their essays at "rough draft" without creating anything memorable to jump off the page, differentiating themselves from other applicants who look like them academically.

    You are not spending minutes or hours staring at a blank page wondering what to write about.

    You are not planning to somehow just "wing it" and get into your dream school.

    Rather, you have arrived at this step knowing exactly what you need to do in order to effectively communicate exactly what you want to say.

    You have chosen to launch your college career in a very thoughtful, practiced, adult way.

    This is something to celebrate because, like it or not, High School You is ending and Your Future Self hasn't arrived yet; the years in between are statistically sound indicators of how your adult life will begin to take shape.*

*The college application process is the ultimate job interview, and most high school students are uncomfortable with the idea of talking about themselves let alone selling themselves. You, v. 2.0 is a short course for high school juniors and seniors to challenge them to create the person they want to be and point that person in the direction they want to go, and also to introduce them to the idea of selling themselves. Visit essaycure.com to learn more (shameless plug).

06 ROUGH DRAFT

YOU DON'T SIT DOWN TO WRITE A ROUGH DRAFT

This is one of the biggest muscle memory challenges you'll feel as you work your way through this instruction: the rough draft writes itself! You don't "sit down to write" a rough draft. Rather, your rough draft naturally comes together as you work your way through the steps in the process.

A rough draft of a college application essay must:

- ✓ open with a lede that piques the reader's interest and motivates the reader to keep reading, clarify what the essay is about, and demonstrate mastery of academic writing protocols;
- ✓ tell a chronological story that leads up to the moment when everything changes and then goes on to show how the writer was transformed by the experience, while weaving in

- elements of personal statements that show what kind of student you would be on their campus; and
✓ assert a thesis statement that answers the question posed by the essay prompt and unifies the entire piece of writing from the reader's perspective.

"Cowgirl-up" my grandpa says with a sarcastic tone. That was one of the first things I learned. That saying was constantly said throughout my life when my grandpa insisted us grandkids could do anything. There were four of us: all girls and all a little apprehensive about the ranch life we had been born into. There was never an easy way out and no was never a choice. No matter what was being asked to do, you did it and put a smile on your face.

Where it all started was when I had to ride horses to gather or move cows. This was something I never wanted to do. Riding horses was something I had a big fear of and was not confident doing. For everyone else in my family, it came naturally. Because of this, I often didn't help or be part of this job. I always felt like I was disappointing my grandpa. But at the end of the day that didn't stop me. I found new ways to get around this fear.

My grandpa was never mad that I didn't feel comfortable doing it. He just expected me to find some other way to contribute. So that's what I did. I rode the four wheeler in front of the pack while calling the cattle that came bolting behind me. This might not have been ideal, but I "cowgirl upped" and got the job done.

There was always work to be done from putting up fences to branding cattle and even calving and lambing. Something was always broken or needing work and that's where us grandkids came in handy. Gramps always had jobs for us to do and there was no telling how long they were going to take. You couldn't go inside till the job was done and there was no cheating in the process. Only the best work would be given approval and counted as a job well done.

My gramps wasn't just any grandpa, he was that one person who inspired me to set my fears aside and preserve. It doesn't matter if you are a girl or boy, young or old: You can do it. It took being on the ranch, overcoming challenges to know what was important to me. It tested every part of me. But in the end I know I can "Cowgirl Up" and get the job done.

He was someone that I feel very fortunate to have in my life. Everyone in their life has people that have impacted them and helped them become who they are, but I don't think anyone has someone like my grandpa.

If you haven't already guessed, this is an example of an essay that begins and ends at *rough draft*. The writer admits this.

RIGHT MY COLLEGE APPLICATION ESSAY

As she worked her way through The Steps in the Righting Process, she learned a few things:

- She took out the "testimonial" to her grandfather and put it in a separate document, one that she presented to him as a thank-you on her high school graduation day.
- She learned that "phrasal verbs" only need to be hyphenated if used as nouns or adjectives; when used as verbs, there's no hyphen.
- She learned that "sarcasm" is a low-level form of anger, and that wasn't the word she was looking to use to describe her motivation to solve a problem to help someone she cares about and respects.
- She learned how to organize her essay, opening with a story that grabbed the reader's attention and later filled in the details of setting (who, what, where, when, why).
- She learned to "show, not tell."
- She learned that her answer to the question in the essay prompt (a significant experience that influenced her life) needed more fleshing out in order to evoke empathy from the reader.
- She learned that the resolution of that experience is her answer to the essay prompt.

She worked in as many noncognitive variables as possible.

She turned writing an essay into an opportunity to weave in a personal statement.

That last bullet point alone is likely the reason she was admitted to her first-choice college; she did more than just simply answer the question; she showed the University of Oregon quite a few things about her personality: she has a strong support system of a family and she has knowledge of working with animals, which is not something she learned in class; she's a hard worker; she's a team player who doesn't want to let her teammates down; she's a problem solver who is able to think critically and outside the box to come up with a solution that meets everybody's needs and expectations; she's not a quitter.

When we put it that way, who wouldn't want a student like this on their campus?

We'll show you her completed essay in a bit.

But first, we need to understand "Navigate" and the concept of what I call "invisible writing."

NAVIGATE

01 RHETORICAL MODE & ORGANIZATIONAL METHOD

02 PREWRITING

03 RESEARCH

04 THESIS

05 OUTLINE

06 ROUGH DRAFT

07 REVISING

08 EDITING

09 FINAL DRAFT

© 2020 Christine Gacharná All Rights Reserved.

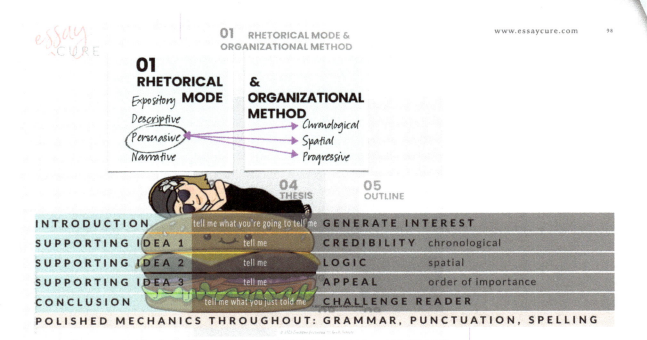

REVIEW: RHETORICAL MODES AND ORGANIZATIONAL METHODS

Let's review how *rhetorical modes* and *organizational methods* fit in with what you might already know:

In high school, you were probably taught to write a common five-point/five-paragraph essay.

The illustration below should help you to visualize a five-point essay.

Although high school teachers often call it a five-point or five-paragraph essay, it's more descriptively a *persuasive* rhetorical mode (also known as *argumentation*) written using the five-point foundation.

In high school, instructors often assign *persuasive* essays to teach students to get an opinion or take a stand.

Using the *persuasive* rhetorical mode to write an essay, the writer introduces the topic and the thesis in the introduction, presents opposing and qualifying ideas and strong evidence in support of these claims, and then wraps things up with a compelling conclusion that restates the topic (subject) and support for the thesis (the writer's premise or opinion on the topic after conducting research).

You may be more familiar with high school teachers explaining it this way: "Tell me what you're going to tell me, tell me, then tell me what you just told me."

Notice that this graphic uses a hamburger bun to represent the introduction and the conclusion? This is no accident. A five-point essay is often illustrated as a hamburger because the buns (introduction and conclusion) communicate the exact same content only in slight variations of words. The meat, lettuce, and cheese of the body paragraphs contain supporting ideas all related to the topic. There's rarely a chocolate chip cookie layered into a hamburger. In the essay world, that would be equally wrong. If the essay topic is aviation, for example, veering off-topic in the third paragraph to talk about grooming a Goldendoodle would be a complete digression and would probably earn the student a lower grade.

I want to pause here because this is the point where I'm used to seeing lightbulbs flash across the faces of a good number of students. Take a moment to go back and start from the beginning of this chapter if you feel your foundation of high school essay writing is iffy at best.

The *persuasive* rhetorical mode is a popular choice among high school teachers and undergraduate instructors because it's a solid foundation upon which to build understanding and mastery of academic writing.

Persuasive essays can use any of the three *organizational methods*: *chronological, spatial,* or *order of importance*, to present ideas and support evidence. This is one of the reasons high school teachers like this rhetorical mode—it gives the student more flexibility in how the information is organized.

Another reason most high school essays are written in the *persuasive* rhetorical mode is to encourage students to begin demonstrating critical thinking (as defined by the essay's thesis).

This is another big lightbulb moment.

The problem with the *persuasive* rhetorical mode is that it's so popular and so common, students start to think all essays look like five-point, hamburger, persuasive essays all of the time. And that is simply not true.

So this is a good time to step back and examine the difference between a topic and a thesis.

> *topic = subject, thesis = premise*
> A thesis is the writer's point of view gleaned from info & research. The thesis what the writer has to say about the topic, a statement or theory that is put forward by the writer as a premise to be maintained or proved.
> *A thesis should be easily stated in 25 words or less.*

REVIEW: TOPIC VS. THESIS

A *topic* is a matter dealt with in a text, discourse, or conversation; it's a *subject*.

A *thesis* is a *statement, theory,* or *premise* that is put forward to be maintained or proved.

topic = subject | thesis = premise

A thesis is the writer's point of view gleaned from information and research.

A thesis is not a topic; rather, a thesis is what the writer has to say about the topic.

Think of it this way:

An essay's topic might be common house pets and the thesis might be, "When it comes to house pets, cats are far superior to dogs."

Or perhaps the thesis will be, "Dogs are far superior to cats as household pets."

Q: Which thesis in that example is the correct thesis?
A: Whichever one the writer can most convincingly support with research and clear, engaging writing to persuade the reader to agree.

Another lightbulb moment there? A *persuasive* essay oftentimes has more than one "right" answer—it's up to the student to find supporting evidence to convince (persuade) the reader one way or the other, using a thesis statement for help. Remember your high school teacher mentioning something about a "working thesis?" That's because thesis statements can be subject to change. Sometimes, after extensive research, the lab tests conducted or the information gathered, synthesized, and evaluated enlighten the student to see the topic from a different direction. A "working thesis" allows students to progress in a direction, but doesn't lock them into that destination if learning uncovers a different avenue.

For example: Let's say a student sets out to convince his teacher that cats are far superior house pets than dogs. This student has never personally owned a dog. In visiting both a local shelter and a pet store, talking with and interviewing employees and neighbors who own dogs, the student learns things that change his mind.

I know that's a ridiculously simplified example, but it illustrates perfectly the whole point of both the purpose of a "working thesis" and how the *persuasive* rhetorical mode got its name.

A thesis should be easily stated in twenty-five words or less.

If it's taking you ten minutes to stumble all over yourself to describe to someone what your thesis is (and even longer to write it), your thesis isn't ready. Generally, when this happens, it's because the student doesn't quite know the material well enough yet to form an opinion.

In college, academic essays will be written around new and complex concepts and ideas. A thesis statement forces a student to think critically about the topic (subject of the essay) and use academic writing, including a thesis, to demonstrate synthesis of learning.

Writing a solid thesis statement helps a student identify what was learned from the instruction in the course. The student isn't necessarily expected to coin the phrases or prove the theories—the discussion and theories are taught in the course! The student is expected, in the essay, to demonstrate knowledge of (thinking and doing) this material and synthesis (understanding and thinking) of learning. The more complex the concepts and ideas, the higher the level of coursework instruction.

By contrast—and this should come as a great relief to students reading this workbook—the framework of an academic essay doesn't change! A *persuasive* essay is the same whether it's used in a high school AP Lit class or a 300-level Economics course at a university. The framework of each *rhetorical mode* and *organizational method* stays the same whether a student attends a private or public college or university in the SEC, Pac 12, Big 10, Coastal Collegiate, Mountain West, Ohio Valley, Ivy League, or any Division I, II, or III school. Once you learn the framework for academic writing, you can free yourself from the stress of "writing" the essay and focus your efforts in the direction that will bring you the biggest return on your investment (See "The 80/20 Rule of Righting").

The one-sentence answer to the prompt that you will put forth in your college application essay will be the same practice deployed in developing thesis statements as you write academic essays in college.

There are no wrong answers to your college application essay prompts. There is only *your* answer, and how well you support that answer determines whether the reader follows along with you and is somehow moved by what you say.

Remember when your English teachers told you, "Show me, don't tell me?" In order to show, your answer needs to reach the limbic system of your reader, evoking an emotional response.

RIGHT MY COLLEGE APPLICATION ESSAY

A thesis statement is declared after the student has researched the topic and come to the conclusion of what the student thinks or believes about the topic. The essay is then written to support this belief. In the case of the college application essay, the bulk of the "research" on the topic is from life experience.

The "research" in the college application essay will be far easier than it will be once you land yourself a seat as an undergrad in a freshman college course. It starts with examining your life experience and concludes with learning about the college or university where the you intend to apply.

So let's go back to the one-ish sentence answer to the question posed by the *prompts (twenty-five words or less)*.

Think of a story from your life that exemplifies the experience you've identified as your thesis, your answer to the question posed by the prompt.

Tell me that story. Begin at the beginning and write out the whole thing, start to finish, in chronological order. Write as fast and furious as you can, leaving nothing out. Don't try to sound smart. Just jot it down (think "freewriting"). The story should use simple, concise construction because that's the rule in academic writing. If you're unsure, imagine you're telling the story to a fourth-grader and use language a fourth-grader would understand. This is not meant as an insult to fourth-graders; rather, it's a guideline professional writers and journalists worldwide adhere to. Remember: the reader of your college application essay very well may speak multiple languages, and English may not be the first. Never put your own filters over your essay, as you will never be the reader.

Some students benefit from dictating this answer into the voice memo of their smartphone and then transcribing it later.

Just as the problem of not wanting to ride horses on her grandfather's ranch became the topic of one student's essay, the solution she found to this problem became the story of her essay that she outlined, wrote, revised, and edited for the application to the college of her dreams.

Yes. She got in. :) But not until after she went through this very same process.

(You'll get to follow the progression of her essay from "starting and ending at rough draft" to RIGHT as you work your way through this workbook.)

Jonathan wrote about how much he hated competitive swimming, avoiding it as a kid by convincing his parents to let him play the saxophone instead, yet was forced as a country club lifeguard to swim a competitive race for the club's team. On the starting block next to him: the star swimmer from his high school. (No pressure.)

The body of Jonathan's essay tells the story of how he overcame this challenge. (*Narrative.*) His unexpected struggle in the one-hundred-yard freestyle gave him a different perspective both in his job as a lifeguard and in his daily life that not every perceived failure equals a life failure, and his future self depends on his failures today (his thesis).

A thesis statement is declared after the student has researched the topic and come to the conclusion of what the student thinks or believes about the topic. The essay is then written to support this belief.

When it comes to the college application essay, most of which are written in the narrative rhetorical mode, the topic will be provided to you.

The topic is the question posed by the essay prompt.

"Reflect on a time when you questioned or challenged a belief or idea. What prompted your thinking? What was the outcome?" *The topic is a time when you questioned or challenged a belief or idea. The thesis statement is your unique answer to describe what prompted your thinking.*

Your goal here is to be unforgettable. You want admissions officers to remember your answer to the question "What was the outcome?" long after they've stopped reading your essay.

Beware: there might be an answer (a thesis statement) that proves a bit more engaging, enlightening, or interesting than others you've tried. Just because you came up with one answer doesn't mean you couldn't come up with another and, after comparing the two or sharing both with friends and family for feedback, feeling that one is much stronger to support than the other, or one is more interesting to read about than the other, or one better answers the scope of the question the essay prompt is asking, or one may lend itself to telling a story that weaves in a personal statement more easily than the other.

Q: How do I find the most engaging answer to the question the essay prompt is asking?
A: I know. This is tough. It requires *thinking*. And *doing*.
Q: Doing what, exactly?
A: Freewriting.

Remember in the beginning when I promised you that this book was not about the writing?

RIGHTING a college application essay is hard work. It's probably the most difficult, most important five hundred words you've ever written. Writing five hundred words isn't hard—RIGHTING five hundred words is hard.

It doesn't start with *rough draft*.

It begins and ends with *you* in the trenches of freewriting exercises. What do *you* have to say about the essay prompt? When that answer comes out, deploy the five layers of why to examine the next answer. Ask *why?* again. Digging down and peeling back the layers of *why?* is grueling for students because it forces you to feel vulnerable and sometimes scared. If you're feeling a bit scared, you're doing the work.

You must figure out what it is you're trying to say before you sit down and try to write it.

This is the RIGHTING (the thinking and the doing) that will separate you from those who look like you academically—those other students who will begin and end with "rough draft" somewhere around Halloween for early action essays that are due November 1.

Take your prewriting exercises seriously. Work hard during those fifteen minutes to question your answers, ask yourself why, stay authentic to yourself in your writing. Take confidence in yourself in this process! Every single student who works at this freewriting exercise writes at least one sentence as a diamond in the rough that later shines to become the base idea for a spectacular essay. If you put in the work, it will happen to you too. You will be surprised by your own brilliance.

When you return to those exercises later, examine them critically.

Are you interested in this topic? Do you think others will find it interesting?

Does it answer the prompt in a way that gives admissions officers an insight into who you are as a person and what you might offer their campus?

Once you have your answer to that, your answer to the essay prompt, the writing simply falls into the formula.

Q: Wait. Did I miss the part where we learned the formula?

A: Fasten your seatbelt. Now that we've convinced you of the importance of Step 1, it's time to level up your game from high school English to academic writing at the undergraduate level.

01 RHETORICAL MODE & ORGANIZATIONAL METHOD

Expository
Descriptive
Persuasive
Narrative

Chronological
Spatial
Progressive

RHETORICAL MODES AND ORGANIZATIONAL METHODS

The first step in the writing process is to choose the *rhetorical mode* and *organizational method*.

Rhetoric is simply a fancy word that puts a name on the art of effective or persuasive speaking or writing. Try substituting "effective speaking" or "persuasive speaking" or "effective writing" or "persuasive writing" for the word "rhetoric," and suddenly it doesn't seem so scary.

You'll begin to hear the word "rhetoric" quite often as both a newly minted voter and college freshman.

Rhetorical modes, therefore, are simply the manner or techniques used to effectively (and sometimes persuasively) communicate through language, especially in writing.

Think of a rhetorical mode as a big picture outline—not the kind of outline with Roman numerals that made your head spin in high school, but rather more like a road map. It's the overall direction that your writing needs to take in order to lead the reader.

An *organizational method* helps us present ideas within each rhetorical mode in an orderly, logical way.

The difference between *rhetorical modes* and *organizational methods* is that *organizational methods* deal more with the specific details of organizing and arranging content. If the *rhetorical mode* is a big-picture Rand McNally glossy 11×17 road map, then the *organizational method* is the detailed Google map directions over the car speakers along the way:

Take La Jolla Pkwy and I-5 S to Damon Ave
Turn right onto La Jolla Shores Dr
Use any lane to turn sharply left onto Torrey Pines Rd
Take exit 23 toward Balboa Ave/Garnet Ave,
Sharp left onto Damon Ave, destination will be on the left, In-N-Out Burger

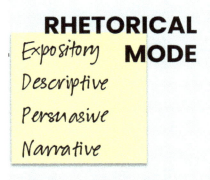

There are many different types of rhetorical modes. The four most common rhetorical modes include *narration*, *description*, *exposition*, and *argumentation*. In this workbook, we're only going to cover *one* of these rhetorical modes, and that's the one you'll need to write your college application essay.

There are three different organizational methods:

1. *Chronological* (time) begins with what happened first, next, and last. It is most often used for narration or explaining how to do something step-by-step.
2. *Spatial* (pronounced Spay-shell] moves across spaces in some specific way, such as from top to bottom, inside to outside, near to far, or left to right, in order to describe something *(The directions above would be an example of spatial order).*
3. *Progressive*, sometimes known as *order of importance*, moves from the least compelling idea to the most compelling idea or vice versa. It is best used for persuading and convincing a reader to think or act in a specific way.

The problem with the *persuasive* rhetorical mode is that it's so popular and so common, high school students start to think all essays look like five-point, hamburger, persuasive essays all of the time. And that is simply not true.

I need you to understand the *persuasive* rhetorical mode:

- is only *one* rhetorical mode;
- is *not* the *only* rhetorical mode;
- is *not* the rhetorical mode you'll use to write your college application essays.

So forget about what you know about five-point hamburger essays and get ready to learn about the *narrative* rhetorical mode and how to use it to Right your college application essay.

Okay, stand up, stretch, take a deep breath. You may want to read this chapter again and allow this information to really sink in and take root. What you just learned is the backbone of academic writing at the undergraduate level.

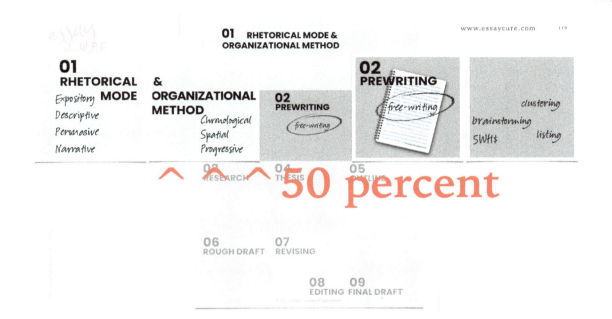

FIFTY PERCENT OF YOUR WORK HAPPENS HERE

The *narrative* rhetorical mode tells a story or narrates an event or a series of events. The college application essay tells a story—your story.

The narrative rhetorical mode in the form of a college application essay organizes ideas around a central conflict.

If there has been no significant change as the result of this conflict, there is no college application essay.

Think about that for a moment because it makes a lot of sense in regard to what you are trying to accomplish: most college application essay prompts ask students to write about an experience where the student learned something significant, valuable, important, relevant.

Your college application essays, then, should be written in the narrative rhetorical mode in order to describe the conflict and how you wrestled its resolution and came out changed on the other side.

Put another way: it's a story about learning and growing as a young person experiencing the human condition. Done right, it's a glimpse into a facet of your character that weaves in a personal statement to describe what kind of person you are.

Remember how we learned earlier that different rhetorical modes use different organizational methods?

The *narrative rhetorical mode* requires *chronological order* whereas, say, *illustration rhetorical mode* requires *order of importance*.

Q: Okay. That kind of makes my head spin. How do I know which rhetorical mode to use, and how do I know which organizational method goes with which rhetorical mode? And which one do I use for my college application essay?

A: Now we're getting somewhere. The fact that you're asking this question means you're starting to understand.

In academic writing, oftentimes the rhetorical mode will be dictated in or by the assignment, and most times the organizational method will be as well. What this means for you is that you don't have to draw from the depths of your soul to write an academic essay! It's academic writing! These compositional techniques are writing's equivalent to the wheel; they are familiar to the reader and they present ideas in a logical, understandable, and predictable way. There's very little artistic license in academic writing. You simply need to decode the assignment and plug the information into the formula.

This should come as a huge relief to most of you: once you figure out which rhetorical mode and organizational method to use, the essay pretty much writes itself. It's the Righting of the essay that needs your attention—the thinking and the doing that comes with following the steps in the process.

Pro tip: For now, what you need to know is that the college application essay follows the *narrative rhetorical mode* and the *narrative rhetorical mode* always uses *chronological order* to organize ideas.

NARRATION + CHRONOLOGICAL

LEDE	JUMP RIGHT IN! GRAB YOUR READER'S HAND & LEAD THEM INTO YOUR STORY.
SET STORY	BACK UP: IDENTIFY WHO, WHERE, WHEN. SET THE SCENE SO THE READER UNDERSTANDS WHERE THEY ARE.
SHOW STORY	TELL YOUR STORY CHRONOLOGICALLY, LEADING UP TO THE MOMENT WHEN EVERYTHING CHANGES.
CLIMAX	SHOW-DON'T-TELL THE MOMENT WHEN EVERYTHING CHANGES.
SHOW CHANGE	DIRECTLY RELATE THE SIGNIFICANCE OF YOUR STORY TO THE QUESTION THE PROMPT IS ASKING.
PERSONAL SIGNIFICANCE	EXPLAIN THE SIGNIFICANCE, VALUE, IMPORTANCE, & RELEVANCE OF COMING TO TERMS WITH RESULTING CHANGE(S) WHICH PERSONIFIES YOUR CHARACTER AND MAKES YOU THE PERSON YOU ARE TODAY
MECHANICS	USE POLISHED GRAMMAR, SPELLING, & PUNCTUATION THROUGHOUT THE ESSAY

Here's the secret sauce:

Narration tells your story (the resolution of conflict) by relaying a chronological series of events in an emotionally engaging way.

Think literature, except in the sense that your story needs to be authentic and true since every college application essay begins and ends with *you*.

It's counterintuitive because in high school, your academic essays have largely been in the persuasive rhetorical mode where everything must be cited, and first-person is not allowed.

In the narrative rhetorical mode, things are different. It's understandable that you feel some muscle-memory pushback as you begin to think in this direction. Stay with me, though, because it's absolutely imperative that you use the narrative rhetorical mode for your college application essay.

All stories have a beginning, a middle, and an end. Just like in persuasive academic essays, transition sentences separate the beginning, middle, and end, so that the reader receives clues of where you're going and is able to follow along.

The *narrative rhetorical mode* unfolds its story in *chronological order* (time), beginning with the events leading up to the conflict and then what happened from there, what happened next, and ends with the final resolution.

Since I'm a professional writer, I teach students to put a slight twist on the college application essay. Once the story is written, chronologically, start to finish, I work with the student to pull out the most interesting, exciting, oftentimes the diamond-in-the-rough sentence from freewriting, and we reorganize the essay by inserting that line at the beginning. Professional writers call this a "lede." It's more commonly known outside writing circles as a hook to get the reader engaged.

The trick to a good lede or hook is to engage the limbic system of the reader's brain.

Q: What does that even mean?
A: It means stringing words together in a way that engages the reader's senses to paint a universal picture using the human conditions of basic emotions.

Pro tip: That's a big idea. Do the best you can to absorb it. For a more detailed explanation, see "Writing is a Complicated Art" in the bonus chapter.

A good lede/hook followed by a narrative essay written in chronological order might look something like this:

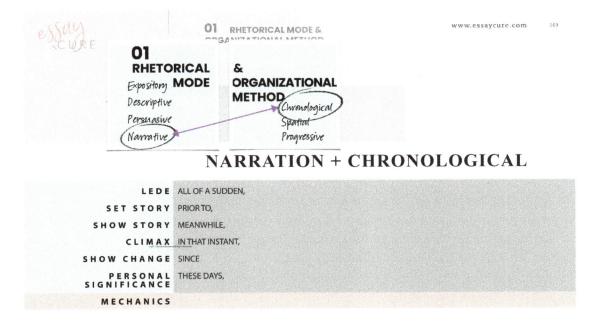

Take a deep breath.

By the time you're finished with this chapter, you've conquered the most difficult part! The first two steps in the process are fifty percent of the work in writing your college application essay.

Writing a rough draft is not the most difficult part of academic writing. By the time you get to rough draft, the essay is mostly written. Using the steps in the process helps you get to that point. That explains why students who sit down to write a rough draft end up staring at the blank page because academic writing isn't about the writing: it's about the *thinking* and the *doing*.

Academic writing does not require students to dig from the depths of their souls to create a *New York Times* best seller. In fact, unless you're applying to study creative writing in the English department or editorial writing in the J-Dept, the college application process (including scholarship applications that include essays) may be the only time you use the narrative rhetorical mode as an undergraduate.

Hopefully, you're starting to see that academic writing follows simple, defined formulas in much the same way algebra follows a formula.

By following the Steps in the RIGHTING Process and understanding and incorporating the correct rhetorical modes and organizational methods, the bulk of the work is finished long before you even get to rough draft.

I train my students to stop asking, "Will you edit this for me?" because editing is the least of an undergraduate student's problems with an essay! You can find someone on the internet for twenty-five bucks to "edit" an essay. Editing is easy.

If you're applying to colleges and universities, you already know how to write. *Stop asking others to edit your essay and focus instead on the content you're trying to communicate.* Use The 80/20 Rule of RIGHTING that you've learned and focus all of your efforts on the sixty percent of the essay that will yield you eighty percent of your results—the content!

Q: Okay. But I'm still not 100 percent sure where to start writing.

A: That's great! If you had started writing by now, you'd be like the guy who pours spaghetti sauce over uncooked noodles. The only writing you should have done so far is the freewriting. The writing part, by the time you get to it, is easy! It's the RIGHTING part (the *thinking* and the *doing*) that's hard.

Up next: Research. (Relax, it's not the citation of sources that was the persuasive essay, and most of the work you've already done even without knowing.)

*Rhetorical modes are explained in depth in the next workbook, *Right My Essay*. One of the reasons I gave you this brief introduction is because if you happen to write yourself into your dream school using our method, said dream school is going to expect that you know how to write academic essays. When writing gets in the way of academic essays, especially at the college level, it can be a tremendous struggle for the student (shameless plug).

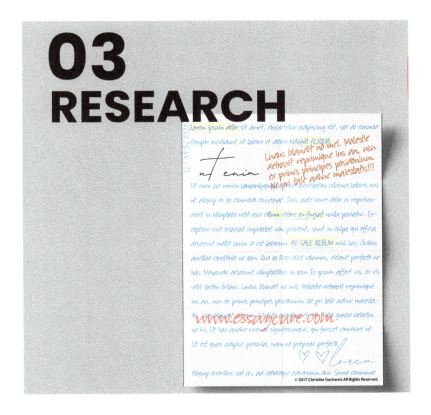

RESEARCH

"Don't dress for the job you have—dress for the job you want."

This advice is often given to college graduates as they go out into the workforce in their shiny new career.

Think about it. The gist of the lesson is to present oneself as a viable candidate for the next step.

Consider your college application essay in the same light. This is your opportunity to showcase your ability to communicate effectively at college-level work—highlight your personality, demonstrate your ability to write well, support a logical argument, or tell a compelling story.

In high school, students often get away with throwing out opinions without first completing the research or fully understanding the new and complex concepts and ideas their teachers are trying to get them to learn.

In college, this doesn't fly.

For example, a college civics professor doesn't want to read an essay that states your opinion about NFL players kneeling during the National Anthem; a college professor wants to read what you think about NFL players kneeling during the National Anthem *as it relates to the chapter of assigned readings on the First Amendment and relevant class discussions.*

See the difference? It's a subtle nuance, but extremely important. It's addressing the details that you went out of your way to absorb to demonstrate synthesis of learning.

Know your audience. I'm certain you've heard your high school teacher say this. In academic writing, your audience is your instructor.

In your college application essay, your audience is admissions officers at the university to which you are applying. They're looking for students who are academically qualified with something unique to bring to their campus community. They want to know who you are and what you can bring to their campus, but they also read *tens of thousands* of essays. They want you to make an effort to be interesting!

Going out of your way to learn involves research.

Since this particular essay may be used by admissions officers to determine whether you are a proper fit for the school, it's in your best interest to research why you are a good fit.

You've already completed the first half of this process by selecting schools for your list that are a good fit for you—now you need to dig deeper, to learn more about why you are a good fit for that school.

Why should admissions officers pick you over other students who look like you academically?

What can you bring to their campus?

Since each school has unique prompts, the research you'll be doing will vary, depending on the school.

Your research might include:

- academics;
- nonacademics;
- student activities;
- specialized instruction.

For example, consider this essay prompt:

"Our families and communities often define us and our individual worlds. 'Community' might refer to your cultural group, extended family, religious group, neighborhood or school, sports team or club, co-workers, etc. Describe the world you come from and how you, as a product of it, might add to the diversity of the University of Washington."

In this essay prompt above, the UW doesn't want to hear what you think you know about diversity in general. The UW wants to hear what you know about diversity *based on what you've learned by going out of your way to investigate diversity on the UW campus in particular, and how you see yourself fitting into that paradigm.*

Your essay, therefore, must reflect your efforts toward research in this direction.

Ahhhhhhhh. Another lightbulb moment?

RIGHT MY COLLEGE APPLICATION ESSAY

You can gather this information by combing through a school's website, searching their Naviance profile (if your school provides you access to this,) or, visiting the campus—ideally, during a formal open house, when each college within the campus and student groups are showcasing academics and student opportunities, or at a bare minimum by combing through the school's website and taking an online tour if available.

Pro tip: You might find in the process of this research that perhaps your one-sentence essay prompt answer/thesis statement isn't as strong in one particular question as it is in another. If that's the case, by all means, choose to answer the questions from the prompts where you feel most confident in presenting your one-sentence answer.

For example, if *showcasing the ways in which you might contribute to the diversity of a campus* leaves you feeling like writing, "Meh. IDK," but *describing a time when you made a meaningful contribution to others in which the greater good was your focus* gives you an opportunity to discuss an extracurricular activity that you learned in your research will also be available to you on their campus, definitely choose the second option.

Remember: the bulk of the "research" in your college application essay is from life experience. The rest of the research is on the college or university where you intend to apply.

OUTLINE

Wait! Before you succumb to the dread that's setting in from memories of English classes of old, let's visualize all of the Roman numerals on the pages of outlines floating up and off, carried right out the window and away with the wind, never to be seen or typed again.

Whew! Wasn't that nice?

It's one of the greatest things about life after high school: if something isn't working for you, you are now the adult in control. You have the power to discard what's not working and replace it with something that does. In college, your life becomes a slate of decisions that *you* get to make! The freedom is intoxicating.

Of course, with freedom comes responsibility. While you have the freedom to make the decisions, you must assume complete responsibility for said decisions. It's a double-edged sword, but it's still pretty cool to behold—especially if it means letting go of those awful Roman numeral outlines and adopting an outline system that actually works for us. Right?

So here we sit with our outlines, sans Roman numerals, A-B-Cs, and 1, 2, 3s. Notice how every step in the writing process leads to the outline? The outline is affected by the completion of every step before it.

Think of an outline as the opening scene of an episode of *The Simpsons*: everyone comes crashing in from all different directions and they all land cohesively on the couch, part of a bigger whole. The outline is the glue that binds an essay. It's the vehicle from which everything is delivered.

Pro tip: Without information to organize and plug into an outline, there can be no rough draft.

College admissions officers and instructors understand this implicitly. For that reason, they can spot immediately a student whose essay begins and ends at rough draft. Think about it: we're more than halfway through the workbook and the process and we haven't even arrived at the rough draft step yet!

REVIEW: FIVE-POINT "HAMBURGER" ESSAY OUTLINE

A typical high school or college-level 5-point persuasive essay might look something like this:

Sample Persuasive Rhetorical Mode Outline

    Introduction: introduce the topic of the essay
    Generate reader interest
    State working thesis in twenty-five words or less

    Organize ideas 1–3 chronologically, spatially, or progressively
    Idea #1 topic sentence
    Idea #1 supporting details (cite references)

    Idea #2 topic sentence:
    Idea #2 supporting details (cite references)

    Idea #3 topic sentence
    Idea #3 supporting details (cite references)

    Conclusion (no new information)
    Signal the end of the essay with transition word(s)
    Summarize the main ideas of interior paragraphs

RIGHT MY COLLEGE APPLICATION ESSAY

Restate the thesis in different words
Look to the future or challenge the reader to take action or make a change

Easy enough, right?

Well, yeah, easy enough if you went to class, took notes, did the assigned readings, and completed the assignments that helped you to learn. It's not possible to incorporate into an academic essay one hundred percent of all information available on any given topic. It's the student's challenge to cull what's needed to demonstrate synthesis of learning as it pertains to the course and instruction.

The thing about academic writing is that the course hands you the content for the essay! The course will have you drinking from a fire hose; as a student, it's your job to sift through all of that information to come up with the ideas that best support your thesis statement based on all the available information.

High school students who go to college thinking they can sleep through class and wing it by writing essays eventually flunk out. Sometimes, those students are eventually able to recover, but not by winging it and sleeping through class. "If you want something you've never had, you need to do something you've never done."

Students who learn to use the proper formula and outline have an advantage: instead of struggling with the "writing," they can focus on the thinking and the doing. Concentrating one's efforts on the content of the essay (i.e., adhering to The 80/20 Rule of Righting) yields far better results (i.e., grades.)

At this point, the writer has already identified a solid topic, dseveloped a working thesis, has enough research to back up the interior paragraphs of the essay, and is preparing to start plugging that information into the outline. The writer might need to retrace his or her steps at any point in this process, by, say, additional research to clarify thoughts or even changing or refining a thesis statement, so that it better lines up with the material as the student writes, or to fill any sections of the outline that appear light or even empty, but for the most part, the hard work is finished.

Our writer is prepared—anxious, almost—to get started on the rough draft.

Let's stop for a moment and think about where this writer stood at the beginning of the process, routinely starting and ending an essay with rough draft. This student sat, often for minutes upon end, staring at the blank page rather than at the thoughts, preparation, class notes, research, information from assigned readings and/or labs, and organization that should be in front of any undergraduate attempting an academic writing assignment.

Which version of this same student would you rather be?

(Hint: Remember, academic writing serves as an assessment and assessments are awarded grades. Your aim in reading this workbook is to be 1) the applicant who gets accepted and then 2) the undergraduate who gets good grades and graduates.)

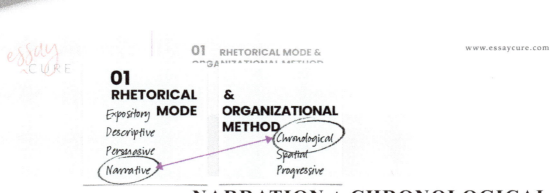

NARRATION + CHRONOLOGICAL OUTLINE

An outline serves to organize ideas.

Here's how the *narrative rhetorical mode* using *chronological order* might look for a college application essay outline:

Remember, we're teaching you to put a slight twist on your college application essay. We do this to grab your reader's attention. We do this to grab the reader's attention; a reader intrigued by the lede or hook won't put the essay down. We're looking to make you jump off the page.

To do this, we're writing a first sentence that engages the reader's senses and paints a universal picture using the human conditions of basic emotions.

A lede or a hook is different from an introduction. We're not writing an introduction here; we're not telling the reader what we're going to tell them. Instead, we're jumping right in with an interesting lede to hook them, grab their interest. See the difference?

Here are some examples of great ledes written by some of my previous students:

I wish you could feel how unbelievably hot it was. One kid passed out.

All of the notes are running away from me off the page.

We turned onto Cispus Street.

RIGHT MY COLLEGE APPLICATION ESSAY

All I can see is a dove.

It was fast and high: a combination for trouble.

Every one of these sentences was a diamond in the rough—a sentence that the student didn't even realize its brilliance while it was buried somewhere in a freewriting exercise. Plucked from the paragraphs and turned into a lede, each one sets the stage for the reader to be curious and want to learn more.

An outline of a good lede/hook followed by a narrative essay written in chronological order might look something like this:

(*Essay prompt goes here.* Include college name and word count restrictions, if any.)

Lede

Begin by describing an interesting detail from somewhere in your story. Jump right into the action. Grab the reader's hand and invite them to join you. Lead them in. Show me, don't tell me. (By default, this will generate reader interest.)

Let's back up here to set the story (chronological).

Identify who, where, when. Set the scene so the reader understands exactly where they are as they walk with you (since the reader is now in the story with you.) Do not wait too long to do this, because readers who feel lost will leave.

Show the story (chronological).

Keep telling the story in chronological order. Lead the reader right up to the moment when everything changes.

Climax (chronological).

This is the moment when everything changed. Without this moment, everything would still be the status quo. This is the moment that needed to happen to you in order for you to emerge on the other side with a new and/or different perspective. Show me, don't tell me.

Show the Change.

Begin where things changed. Show, don't tell, the events that happened as a result of the moment where everything changed.

Another way to think of this scene is a description of how things are today and why they are different as a result of the climax.

Personal Significance (no new information).

What's the point? Explain the significance, value, importance, relevance of coming to terms with the resulting directly to your answer to the question the essay prompt is asking. Somewhere in here should be a one-sentence statement that delivers your answer to the essay prompt.

That's it!

Copy and paste the outline tailored to the college application essay into a blank document.

Go back to one of your freewriting assignments from this particular topic/prompt. Copy and paste any of the phrases or ideas you've written so far that work to fill in the blanks of the outline, keeping them arranged in chronological order except for the lede.

Review your research; does any of the research from this particular university/prompt fall into this story? If so, plug it into its chronological place.

Keep filling in the sections of the outline using ideas and phrases from the freewriting and details from research.

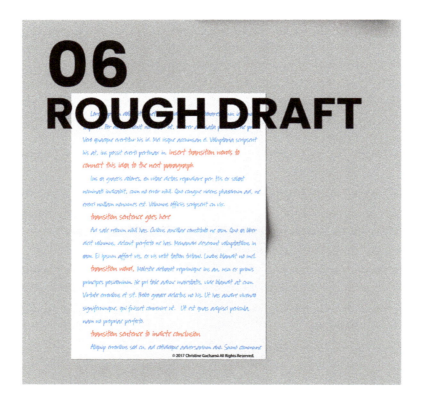

ROUGH DRAFT

Let's review how the student who came from a ranching family, but didn't like riding horses went from starting and ending at rough draft in her first essay to following the steps in the process to contribute to a thoughtful and purposeful essay draft.

After going back to the drawing board and completing the exercise on freewriting, she was able to plug her words into an outline to build the framework of a rough draft:

LEDE. Jump right in.
"Cowgirl up!" Gramps has been saying to us since I can remember.
SET THE STORY. Identify who, what, where so your reader understands where they are
It seems I'm the only one who is a bit apprehensive of ranch life.
I don't like riding horses. For everyone else in my family, it seems to come easy.
Plus, Gramps expects everyone to pitch in and help.
Off they would go.
Everybody left without me and I had to sit in the house alone.

RIGHT MY COLLEGE APPLICATION ESSAY

I was disappointing Gramps and I felt left out.
I didn't like being separated from the rest of my family.
They were all out doing something for the day.
Climax. Show-don't-tell the moment when everything changes.
At dinner, they'd laugh and tell stories.
Find some other way to contribute.
I learned how to ride the four-wheeler.
Show Change. Continue to show (don't tell) the story (chronological order).
Putting up fences, branding cattle, calving, and lambing—there's always something to do.
Something was always broken or needed to be fixed.
Personal Significance. Explain the significance, value, importance, and relevance of coming to terms with the resulting change(s) that personifies your character and makes you the person you are today. Remember, if there's been no significant change, there isn't much of a college application essay.
I found a new way to get around my fear.
End the Story (no new information)
I found a way to "cowgirl up" and get the job done.

At this point, writing the rough draft is nothing more than taking the sentences in the outline, fleshing out the ideas to fill in the details, and creating transitions from one idea to the next.

Is it any wonder that students who begin and end at rough draft struggle so much with writing assignments?

The rough draft is not the most difficult step in the writing process.
The writing process is most difficult when a writer starts and stops at rough draft.
If you are struggling with writing your rough draft, it's time to go backward, not forward.

Don't worry. Lots of students start again at this point and most of them find their next attempt is far more successful than their first try.

Set a timer for fifteen minutes and freewrite on your topic.

Review the organizational method and rhetorical mode (I've already incorporated this into the outline for you).

Research the school you're applying to. Is there anywhere in your outline where you can plug some of this research in?

State a one-sentence (twenty-five words or less) answer to the essay prompt.

Review the outline formula and plug in sentences and ideas from freewriting, research, and your thesis statement.

Review the list of noncognitive variables. Are you able to work any that apply to you into this story?

REVIEW: PUTTING IT ALL TOGETHER TO TELL YOUR STORY

Tell your story. How?

Start with what happened first.

Keep telling the story. What happened next?

Lead the reader right up to the moment where everything changed.

Show, don't tell, the moment everything changed. Close your eyes and describe the details.

Show, don't tell: the events that happened as a result of the moment everything changed.

Show, don't tell: the final scene and how it directly relates to the question the prompt is asking.

Directly answer the question.

Show the significance, value, importance, and/or relevance of coming to terms with this resulting change.

Now, take the most interesting line(s) from the moment everything changed, and move it to the top of your essay. This is your lede and will get your reader's attention. Invite and entice your reader to keep reading.

Immediately under the interesting first lines of your essay, back up. Identify who these people are, where you were, when, why you were there, how this whole scene came to present in your life. You are setting the scene, so the reader understands exactly and can follow you through the rest of the chronological events.

Keep telling the story. Give the reader vivid details of the moment when everything changed so that readers feel as if they are walking through this with you.

Write your one-sentence answer to the question the essay prompt is asking.

Explain to the reader why this event changed you.

Now go do something else!

Come back to your essay, later, with a fresh set of eyes to continue revising and editing.

Once you feel you have a decent rough draft, show your essay to someone you trust. Don't ask them to edit your essay. Ask instead, "How's my content?"

07 REVISING

REVISING

Q: What's the difference between revising and editing?
A: Revising falls under "Navigate." Editing falls under "Punctuate."

The revision process reshapes the content of your essay, if necessary. Once you've finished with revisions, your essay should be unified—each idea in each paragraph should clearly belong and make logical sense. Your ideas should build on each other in a coherent way. Your changes might be moderate or major, but you want to come out of this process with an essay that is ready for its final styling: editing.

Revising involves moving text around. Revising is big-picture organization; moving sentences or paragraphs to ensure the body of writing "flows" from beginning to end, holding the reader's hand and leading them through with you.

Editing, by contrast, is the nitpicky art of English grammar, punctuation, and spelling. It's last, and we're still not there yet, so continue to not worry about it.

Revising consists of revisiting the draft to review and, if necessary, reshape its content. This stage involves moderate and sometimes major changes: adding or deleting a paragraph, phrasing the main point differently, expanding on an important idea, reorganizing content, and so forth.

Revising means paying particular attention to unity (a quality in which all the ideas in a paragraph and in the entire essay clearly belong and are arranged in an order that makes logical sense) and coherence (a quality in which the wording clearly indicates how one idea leads to another within a paragraph and from paragraph to paragraph).

Here's an example of how revising can completely change the punch and effectiveness of an essay. Can you spot the difference?

> *I love gaming. Fifteen guys from my senior class have a group text meet-up for gaming. It's not my regular group of friends, and the only thing predictable about the game is that today will be completely different from any other.* When any combination of us meet up inside a game, we don't follow the rules. In fact, we try to be absurd as possible, setting unrealistic challenges and goals and creating ridiculous restrictions that lead into sub-games. One example of a game-within-a-game that we play is "line patrol" where one player does everything he can to stop the others from crossing a randomly placed line. We award one another points for imagination and creativity when defining the sub-game rules. One of my favorite aspects of playing familiar games with these offbeat rules is that I interact with people I'd otherwise not normally hang out with at school. Guys from all different walks of our senior class come together to play—athletes, honor students, and every other group in between. Our gaming community is almost like a world of its own. (181 words)

> *It's not my regular group of friends, and the only thing predictable about the game is that today will be completely different from any other. Fifteen guys from my senior class have a group text meetup for gaming.* When any combination of us meet up inside a game, we don't follow the rules. In fact, we try to be absurd as possible, setting unrealistic challenges and goals and creating ridiculous restrictions that lead into sub-games. One example of a game-within-a-game that we play is "line patrol" where one player does everything he can to stop the others from crossing a randomly placed line. We award one another points for imagination and creativity when defining the sub-game rules. One of my favorite aspects of playing familiar games with these offbeat rules is that I interact with people I'd otherwise not normally hang out with at school. Guys from all different walks of our senior class come together to play—athletes, honor students, and every

other group in between. Our gaming community is almost like a world of its own. (178 words)

A new look

It's time to read your paper as if you had never seen it before. This is where it pays off in dividends to write your essays weeks before they are due—it's the easiest way to afford yourself the time needed to come back to it with a more critical eye and make the revisions that bring it closer to your version of perfect.

Sorry, procrastinators. The steps in the writing process don't favor you—and college admissions officers know it.

Picture a college admissions officer who has read tens. Of thousands. Of essays.

Will yours stand out? Will it hold his or her attention? Does it flow? Is it unique? Do your ideas build on each other? Is your essay organized? Does it reach a satisfying conclusion?

Revising is where you become your own critic—the kind of objective critic where you scrutinize your work to make it better, not the kind where you become anxious or you beat yourself up or rate your essay with one star out of five and give up. (If I know anything about my students at this point, it's that your essay likely already rates higher than one star. So you've got that going for you.)

Having said that, this is the time for you to be completely honest with yourself about your work. Here are some tips:

Walk away.

Take a break from your work.

You can't revise too close to the writing process, or else you won't see its flaws. Have you ever been critical of something you've written—or a photograph you've taken or anything you've created—and then found it again sometime later?

Often, with the distance, you'll realize it was better than you thought at first.

Or, you'll see that it was actually nowhere near as good as you once thought it was.

Either way, looking over our work with a fresh set of eyes ensures we'll see it much more clearly for what it truly is. Let it rest for a day or so. Give yourself time in the application process for revision.

View your essay in a different way from how you wrote it. The easiest way to do this is to print it out and read it on paper, with pen in hand.

Another effective way to do this is to read it out loud.

Share it with someone whose circle you aspire to be in to see if your points are understood or if something you've written raises unanswered questions.

Change things up to see what works for you. You'll notice things that you might have missed when you wrote it.

As we noted earlier, part of the revising process means being able to take an objective look at your work with an eye to improving it. Being able to note the essay's strengths and weaknesses is one way of being objective. Can you come up with a strong title to sum it up and capture an admission reader's attention? If not, you might need to use this step to get it back on track. Fix your weaknesses and play to your strengths.

Organize your essay.

Yes, you've already done this. Now you're looking at it one final time to make sure your writing accomplishes what you want it to.

Is a better conclusion hidden higher in the essay?

Do you need to shift some points around to make it stronger?

What questions come up as you read it with a fresh eye? You might need to answer these questions before moving on to your next point.

Do your transitions flow smoothly, or are they abrupt and awkward? You don't want your transitions to slow down the reader; instead, you want them to encourage the reader to keep going.

Make sure you've answered the essay's prompt. Read the question again, and then read your answer to it. Tailor your essay to the prompt.

Check your conclusion. Make sure it ends on a solid, satisfying note. You don't want it to fizzle out as if you were ready to be done with the thing. If it feels like that, look for your conclusion hiding elsewhere in your essay. A simple rearrangement of thoughts might be all it takes to finish it.

Punctuate

01 RHETORICAL MODE & ORGANIZATIONAL METHOD

02 PREWRITING

03 RESEARCH   **04** THESIS   **05** OUTLINE

06 ROUGH DRAFT   **07** REVISING

08 EDITING   **09** FINAL DRAFT

© 2020 Christine Gacharná All Rights Reserved.

08 EDITING

EDITING

People notice typos when they are totally absorbed in the material and shocked by the error. If your reader is lost in the brilliance of the content of your essay, the typos are a nuisance. If the content and organization are a mess, the typos become an affirmation of the reader's distrust, the proverbial nail in the coffin.

Editing's primary client is words. Its job is purely the mechanics of grammar, spelling, and punctuation.

Editing involves making changes to improve style and adherence to standard writing conventions; for instance, replacing a vague word with a more precise one, or fixing errors in grammar and spelling, or correcting punctuation mistakes, or double-checking usage of commonly misused words.

An essay becomes a polished, mature piece of writing in the editing process. This is the end product of the writer's best efforts.

Check for:

- Spelling
- Capitalization
- Punctuation
- Grammar
- Sentence structure
- Subject/verb agreement
- Consistent verb tense
- Word usage

Run spell-check. In this day and age, it's sloppy not to.

Print it out—you'll notice details on paper that you won't see from your computer screen.

Read separately for spelling and grammar errors. It helps to read backward and out loud.

Pro tip: Use commas correctly. Here's a short list of the biggies:

Use a comma after an introductory phrase or clause.

Use commas before and after a parenthetical phrase or clause.

Use a comma to separate two independent clauses linked by a coordinating conjunction (and, but, for, nor or, so, yet)

Learn to use an Oxford comma to avoid ambiguity or unintended interpretations.

Q: What's an Oxford comma?
A: An Oxford comma is the comma used after the penultimate item in a list of three or more items, before "and" or "or." Jimmy got accepted into Cal Tech, Harvey Mudd, and Cornell. The comma before "and Cornell" is the Oxford comma.

Q: Do punctuation marks belong inside or outside of quotation marks?
A: The period and the comma always go inside quotation marks. The dash, the semicolon, the exclamation mark, and the question mark go inside when they apply to the quoted matter (if it's not the entire sentence), but outside when they apply to the whole sentence.

Remember, show me, don't tell me? To be effective at showing, use active verbs. Adjectives and adverbs "tell." Adjectives and adverbs weaken writing by telling, not showing.

Be specific. "Fragrant purple irises" only costs you one more word than "beautiful flowers" and it evokes two senses rather than none. Remove adjectives and adverbs and replace them with specifics that activate your reader's limbic system.

If you don't know a colon from a semicolon, don't use either.

Don't be married to your words.

RIGHT MY COLLEGE APPLICATION ESSAY

The brilliant anecdote that you shared in your essay might be just that—too brilliant for this venue. That kind of brilliance might be too distracting from your essay's thesis or answer to the question posed by the prompt. If it doesn't contribute to your thesis, it can't survive the cut.

Seasoned writers know not to get to attached to their words; they want each word or anecdote to contribute to the whole more than they want to hang on to one example or sentence that doesn't fit.

Nobody—not you, not any college admissions officer—will miss a well-written albeit ill-placed sentence.

Yes, it's painful, but they're only words. Let them go.

Check your facts.

Make sure every statement you make in your essay is true and that you can back up these facts with sources, preferably more than one. This is an important enough step that many magazines and other publications hire fact-checkers to do this full-time—and pay them a salary. Be your own best fact-checker. One wrong fact undermines the integrity of the entire essay. There may not be numerous hard facts and data in a personal essay, but you want every word you write to be unequivocally true.

Word choice. Do you reuse the same words throughout? Can you find a more engaging word that means the same thing without sounding highbrow or awkward?

Are you using texting slang? If so, don't.

Is there a single word that you can use in place of a phrase? Tighten up your writing now to help yourself with word count restrictions later.

Determine your voice.

Make sure your voice is consistent throughout the essay. Don't switch between first-, second- or third-person narrators. Keep an audience in mind and write for that audience throughout the essay. Keep your verb tenses consistent.

The five parts of a *complete sentence* are *capital letter, subject (noun), predicate (verb), complete thought,* and *terminal punctuation* (period, question mark, or exclamation point).

All English words fall into eight categories called parts of speech: *nouns, pronouns, verbs, adjectives, adverbs, prepositions, conjunctions, and interjections.*

A gerund (a noun derived from a verb that ends in "-ing") takes a single subject, so look at those closely. A sentence like "Checking your copy for punctuation and grammar mistakes is essential" takes a singular verb for the subject: "checking." The sentence "Checking and double-checking your copy for punctuation and grammar mistakes are essential" has two subjects and requires the plural "are" (checking and double-checking).

English requires that the general rule of subject-verb agreement be followed at all times. This rule states that *if a verb in a sentence is singular, its subject must also be singular, and if a verb is plural, its subject must also be plural.* If your sentences are too long, it is easy to mess this up. In long sentences, your subject and verb might get separated and convoluted to the point that they don't agree, and you might even evoke antecedent problems by then.

Q: Ugh. What's an antecedent again?
A: At this point, just break your sentence into two parts.

In fact, if your sentence is longer than three lines, consider breaking it up.

Here are some of my pet peeves as I read through student essays:

If you take nothing else from me, take this: avoid sarcasm—in your college application essay, in academic writing, and probably in life in general.

No matter how cute it looks on your Bitmoji, sarcasm is a low-level form of anger.

Sarcasm is literally "the use of irony to mock or convey contempt."

Okay, so first of all, "mock" or "convey contempt" have no rightful place in your college application essay or in academic writing. Or in life. It's not only mean, it's a low-level form of anger, meaning you're saying far more about yourself by using it than you're saying about the person, event, or organization you're trying to cut down.

That should convince you (and believe me, it will convince many of your intellectual peers, the same ones you're competing with for seats in the freshman class), but in the event it doesn't, consider this:

Sarcasm is "*the use of irony* to mock or convey contempt."

Most high school seniors haven't yet mastered the use of irony, let alone the definition. Irony is like a semicolon; if you don't fully understand it and/or know how to use it correctly, best just to avoid.

Please don't confuse sarcasm with wit. Wit means "mental sharpness and inventiveness, keen intelligence, and a natural aptitude for using words and ideas in a quick and inventive way to create humor."

Witty kids are smart and funny. Sarcastic kids are contemptible.

Don't be a sarcastic student (end rant).

"Currently" is almost always redundant. If "I am currently reading," then "I am reading." Avoid using whenever possible.

"Over" is a preposition. It should never be used if your intended meaning is the pronoun determiner "more than."

"Literally" means that exactly what you say is true. "I'm literally dying of shame" means that everything else you tell me from here on I'm not buying. "Literally" literally means no metaphors or analogies.

Everything else is figurative.

Homophones like "your" and "you're" or "they're," "their," and "there" won't show up in a spell check. Check and double-check to verify you are using the intended word. Reading sentences backward and out loud helps with this.

Affect vs. effect: The easiest way to remember the difference between the two is that "affect" means "to make a difference to" or "touch the feelings of (someone); to move emotionally."

(Lightbulb moment)

RIGHT MY COLLEGE APPLICATION ESSAY

Q: Isn't the whole purpose of a college application essay to reach the limbic system of the reader?
A: Yes.

Impact as a noun *and* as a verb literally means forcible contact. A plane crashes on impact. It pains me to write that sentence, as so many people I know and love are out there as we speak flying those planes. It makes me bristle to hear the word "impact" used (which conjures up images of a plane crash) where the word "affect" is sooooooooo much more appropriate and meaningful.

"Impact on" is a phrasal verb. Phrasal verbs are like semicolons; if you don't already explicitly know what it is, and whether or not to hyphenate it, you shouldn't be using it—unless it's integral to your story (like "cowboy up!").

Speaking of hyphenated words: any time you use two adjectives to describe a noun, they must be hyphenated. For example, "the University of Arizona is my first-choice college."

Their, *they're*, and *there*: Use "there" when referring to a location, "their" to indicate possession, and "they're" when you mean to say "they are."

The dismissive "I could care less" is incorrect. If you could care less about it, then you're saying you could care less about the topic, and you've failed to effectively make your point. To use this phrase correctly, insert the word "not" after the word "could," as in, "I could not care less."

Irregardless. This word doesn't exist. The word you should use is "regardless."

A book is "titled." Select recipients are "entitled."

If you mean to say "you are," the correct word is "you're." Use "your" when referring to something that belongs to "you," as in "your first-choice college."

Fewer vs. *less*. Another common mistake, "less" refers to quantity and "fewer" to a number. For instance, Facebook has fewer than five thousand employees, but I got less sleep than your mom did last night and it's really starting to affect me. (See what I did there?)

Do not confuse it's with its. *It's* is a contraction of the words *it* and *is*. *Its* is a possessive pronoun.

It's cold and rainy outside. (It is cold and rainy outside.)

The cat was chasing its tail. (The cat was chasing the tail that belongs to the cat.)

When in doubt, substitute the words "it is" in a sentence. If it works, use the contraction "it's."

After a colon, capitalize the first word in a complete sentence.

Be consistent. Use only one space between sentences.

Whew!

At this point, you've said what you intended to say (COMMUNICATE), adhered to the logical flow of presenting your story by using the correct rhetorical mode and organizational method (NAVIGATE), and polished your presentation (PUNCTUATE).

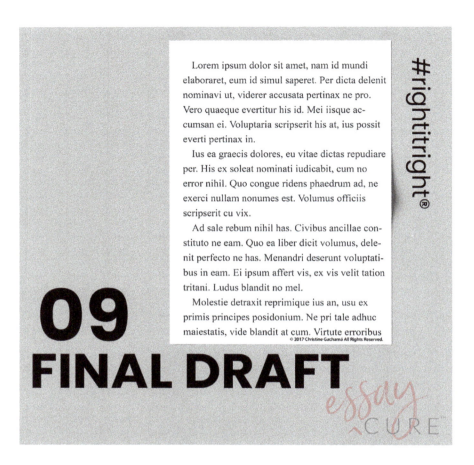

FINAL DRAFT

You're ready to approach others for feedback.

Pick a trusted adult and hand this person a printed version of the final draft of your essay. (They'll see it differently if it's printed, and you're more likely to get it back.) If you're sitting in front of them as they read it, watch their reaction. The opportunity to get a genuine reaction from someone reading your words is a gift.

Whoa, Tiger.

Your polished essay isn't ready for submission—yet.

Not every essay requires this final step, but many undergraduate essays do and almost all college applications do.

Up next: word count.

WORD COUNT

How many times have you dragged a too-heavy backpack to school, or completely overpacked for an overnight stay?

The same applies to writing—it takes time to write short and tight.

Twitter made an entire industry of it.

Many professional writers write what the content is worth and then go back to make cuts to adhere to word count restrictions.

Here are some tips to immediately tighten your writing:

- Prepositional phrases almost always add unnecessary words.
- Use strong, descriptive nouns.
- Use strong, active verbs instead of linking verbs such as "is" or "are."
- Don't start sentences with "There is" or "there are."
- Delete words like "very" or "really" or "currently."
- Question your use of the word "that" as often you can delete it without losing meaning.
- Watch transition words like "in order to," "because of that," "however," and more. Are they necessary?

Q: *I worked my way through this checklist and my essay is still above the stated word count. Can you help me?*

A: Yes. Word count service is available via an ESSAY CURE editor. In this service, we will *not* edit for content, organization, or mechanics! We will simply make the suggested word cuts to help you satisfy that requirement. Visit essaycure.com for more information.

Your very last task will be to look over our suggestions and make sure the essay is still an authentic representation of your voice and of what you wish to say.

FEEDBACK VS. CRITICISM VS. EDITING

There is only one way to avoid criticism: Do nothing, say nothing, and be nothing.
—Aristotle

When people talk, listen completely. Most people never listen.
—Ernest Hemingway

College is a time when you'll be challenged to open your mind to new and complex concepts and ideas.

It's a time when you'll meet people you wouldn't have otherwise gotten to know and get exposed to activities that stretch you outside your comfort zone. This is a time when the *ah-ha* moments will likely change your opinions, spark new ideas, and create a version of you that you haven't even met yet.

Remember earlier when we talked about how to dress for the job we want rather than for the job we have?

It's the same principle.

An earlier version of you, before you discovered this workbook, might ask someone to edit your essay. Now you understand that editing is the final step in the writing process, and you understand why you don't want to be that student.

Q: What if I show someone my essay after all this work and that person criticizes it mercilessly?
A: Good question. Let's break that down and figure out what to do with it.

"Criticism" as a noun has two meanings:

1. The expression of disapproval of someone or something based on perceived faults or mistakes: *he received a lot of criticism | he ignored the criticisms of his friends.*
2. The analysis and judgment of the merits and faults of a literary or artistic work: *alternative methods of criticism supported by well-developed literary theories.*

RIGHT MY COLLEGE APPLICATION ESSAY

The first meaning builds grit and character. The people I know who are the most successful in life are also the people who are surrounded by criticism—and they don't back down, change their opinion, or alter their paths because of criticism.

In fact, what I've observed is this: the most successful people expect critics to emerge—and welcome them. Criticism doesn't tear successful people down. On the contrary, it tends to make successful people contemplate and evaluate, producing insightfulness and growth.

Your question above refers to the first meaning, but really, we should be talking about the second meaning when discussing written works, including your college application essay. "The analysis and judgment of the merits and faults of a literary…work" and therein lies the key: *You're asking for feedback on words on a page—not feedback on who you are as a person or what you may offer the world.*

This is a biggie for two reasons:

1. If what you hear as feedback sounds a little bit like criticism, your first instinct will be to bristle.
2. If you bristle at feedback, your instinct may prod you to defend your work and your defensiveness may (a) shut the feedback down and/or (b) make it impossible for you to hear the valuable feedback you requested.

If you're not open to feedback, then you're not curious and you're not going to be able to improve.

So let's take this idea of "valuable feedback," break down the muscle memory associated with feedback, and apply it to your college application essay and the person you are striving to become.

Jim Rohn says we are the product of the five people we spend the most time with.

Find someone from outside that circle to ask for "feedback" on your essay. Choose teachers from core disciplines who once gave you an "F," a coach who cut you from the varsity team, or an over-achieving sibling. Choose professionals who are not friends with your parents or don't appear on your short list of people who readily deliver your needed feel-good dose of self-esteem.

(Just to clarify, we're not talking about choosing physically or emotionally abusive people. That's an altogether different definition of criticism and one that is never helpful under any circumstance.)

As you seek valuable feedback on what you've written, these people may point out something you haven't yet considered or seen.

Was it interesting?

Was it memorable?

Was there anything in there that made them bristle or question your integrity or intent?

When these people return your essay with their feedback, it's important that you do two things: (1) listen and (2) find the relevant and inherent value in their feedback and incorporate it.

I have one more thing to say about feedback vs. criticism:

The people who will prove to be your biggest cheerleaders in this endeavor are not all likely to be in your circle of Jim-Rohn five.

In fact, the people who prove to be your strongest source of support might not be the people you live with, the people you love, or the people who love you most.

When I was teaching college essay writing to working adults, what I saw most often is that the closer they got to their goal of a college degree, the more pushback they would get from the people in their inner circle.

"You're spending so much time at school, you're so busy, you're always doing homework, what about me, what about us, what about what about what about?"

It's an interesting dynamic. Entire books have been written on it.

I'm not going to dive too deep into it here; you can learn more about it on your own if you are curious and this interests you.

I just want you to be aware that if you have ambitions toward a college degree, and you're working on your essays, planning for your future, and daring to take the initiative to orchestrate your own dreams, don't be surprised if you start to feel some pushback from the people in your inner circle.

Don't let it stop you either if it's what you really want for yourself.

And don't interpret that pushback as unloving. Remember, it's often those who love us most who push the hardest. Therefore, it's especially important for you to find people outside your circle to share your essay with and ask for feedback. Remember: you're not asking them to edit this essay for you. You're asking, "Will you give me your feedback?" and, "How's my content?"

And then brace yourself, recalibrate muscle memory, bite your tongue, and allow yourself to hear the value in the feedback you receive.

Bonus

*We see
the brightness
of a new page
where everything yet
can happen."*
—Rainer Maria Rilke

THE BLANK PAGE

We see the brightness of a new page where everything yet can happen.
—Rainer Maria Rilke

How much time do you spend sitting in front of a blank Word document before you begin to write?
Give me a number. Write it down.
Ten minutes? Twenty minutes? Thirty?

*****

College freshmen write an average of 92 pages per year.*
College seniors write an average of 146 pages per year.
In my experience teaching college essay writing, the average student admits to spending at *least* ten minutes starting at the blank page before committing anything about the assignment to writing. Many admit to spending thirty minutes or more.

Let's just say, for argument's sake, that the average college freshman spends ten minutes staring at the blank page. Ninety-two times.

That's 920 minutes on the low end of the scale. Nine hundred twenty minutes equals *fifteen hours*.

Students who routinely spend thirty minutes staring at the blank page commit a whopping 2,760 minutes—or forty-six hours—of unpaid time to the task.

This time misspent adds up. The student work study program at Northwestern University pays $10/hour; the bookstore at Virginia Tech pays students $12/hour. A fifteen-hour part-time job can earn a student $150–$180. Forty-six hours is akin to a full-time workweek, or $460–$552 of part-time work.

And that's just freshman year.

What would you do with an entire day if you had no school, no work, no practice, no family obligations, or no curfew? Now we're talking real chunks of time—life changing blocks of opportunity and adventure!

Imagine your school, your teachers, your coach, your boss, and parents all gave you an entire day to spend however you wish this week—no conflicts, no issues, all expenses paid. What would you do with that time? Why?

We'll come back to your answer later.

*****

My whole life has been about filling a blank page: school, publishing internships, emails, newspaper reporting, more school, newspaper editing, website building, freelance writing, photography, blogging, social media, Tweets, watercolor class…

I happen to love this stuff.

However, not everybody is as excited about this as I am. I've been learning from aspiring engineers, nurses, business majors, accountants and/or mathematicians that not only is there widespread and vehement distaste out there for the blank page, there also exists a dark place of fear and uncertainty.

If "dark place of fear and uncertainty" resonates with you, then you're in the right place. I'm here to show you how to face the blank page with confidence and purpose.

In order to face the blank page with confidence and purpose, students must first learn to utilize all nine steps in the writing process. As students become proficient in choosing the proper rhetorical mode and organizational method and working their way through the steps in the writing process, the essential elements to success in academic and professional writing pursuits begins to flow effortlessly onto the page.

Facing The Blank Page is the first step toward eliminating fear of or tendency to procrastinate writing tasks.

Facing The Blank Page eliminates the time spent staring at a document and instead hands that time to the writer on the back end, once the essay is completed. Imagine all the things that can be done with this time!

Facing The Blank Page means embracing—not blowing off—the first step in the writing process.[1]

---

[1] National Survey of Student Engagement, an annual survey done at 1,300 four-year colleges every year, looks at the type of work that college freshmen and seniors do. The 2008 survey found that first-year students, on average, wrote 92 pages during the academic year, while seniors wrote 146 pages. For freshmen, the majority of these papers were around five to ten pages, with some first-year students writing papers twenty pages or more.

FACING THE BLANK PAGE

> It is a tremendous act of violence to begin anything. I am not able
> to begin. I simply skip what should be the beginning.
>
> —Rainer Maria Rilke

I learned by accident how to face The Blank Page.

I was twenty-four, working in Arizona as a newspaper reporter. My deadline was 11:00 a.m., at which time I had to submit seven stories to my editor.

Surprisingly, 10:59 a.m. was the most satisfying time in that job. I might still be frantically revising and editing, but my work was, for the most part, finished. The pages were filled.

By 11:01 a.m., the relief of the filled page had evaporated. Instead of the weight of deadline just lifted, I felt the crushing stare of The Blank Page in the next issue's deadline now officially looming. It was this unending writing-on-deadline cycle of my first real job after college that introduced me to both The Blank Page and, more importantly, facing it.

*****

Like all writing, newspaper writing follows a formula. Following a formula for writing is a lot like following a recipe, and anybody can follow a recipe. If one can read, one can cook.

Academic writing also follows formulas.

As a newspaper reporter, the majority of the stories I wrote fell under the "hard news" category, a formula that uses the "inverted pyramid" organizational method. Under this formula, I had to address the who, when, what, where, why, how (and I also tried to include how much $) of a news event, and I had to get as much of that as possible in the beginning of the story.

The reason newspaper stories were written this way is that back in the days when people still read the news on paper, there was a finite amount of space for the printed words. When editors had to make cuts to our stories to fit them into the space allowed, they cut from the bottom up. Thus, the most pertinent information had to stay at the top to avoid getting cut.

Think of it as (duh) an inverted pyramid:

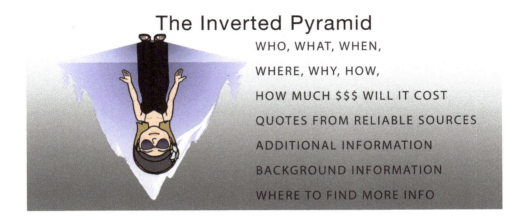

Once a week or so, I'd write a feature story, a style that follows a completely different rhetorical mode and organizational method.

Academic writing uses completely different rhetorical modes and organizational methods from newspaper writing.

While rhetorical modes and organizational methods are important to recognize and understand when writing, don't get too hung up on that detail just yet. We'll get there.

Sometimes, in trying to write my news and feature stories, I'd sit and stare at a blank Word .doc for a long while. Then I'd add my byline at the top, and I'd stare some more. It was much the same experience as lying awake in the wee hours of the morning watching the minutes, and then hours, click closer to the time when the alarm rings.

And then one afternoon, while I was staring at my name on an otherwise blank page, a source returned my call. Since I happened to be sitting at my desk, and since I can type faster than I can write, I tapped my notes from the interview into the already opened Word document as the conversation was taking place.

After I hung up, I looked at the page and OMG (only back then, we didn't have OMG; it was probably more like *voila*)!

That was the moment I discovered the first and most valuable step in the writing process that I learned as an undergrad (but never actually used) truly works: the prewriting strategy of freewriting.

It wasn't a polished version to submit to my editor, but suddenly there were an awful lot of words to work with. The page was no longer blank, and I was no longer staring; I was ~~writing~~ RIGHTING.

My workflow forever changed that day. I didn't have a laptop back then (this was the early '90s—*Wait!* See what I did there? I used an apostrophe to indicate the omission of "19" from 1990, but I did *not* use an apostrophe to separate 1990 from the "s" because *1990s* is plural, not possessive.)

And if there is one mistake students routinely and consistently make in a college application essay, it's getting the apostrophe wrong in years. Those of you who have read this far now know better.

*****

It was the '90s. I didn't have a laptop back then, so most times, my notes were taken with a reporter's notebook and pencil. However, on this day, my notes were already on the page, and *poof!* my interview was most of the content I needed to Communicate in my story.

From there, I'd start cutting and pasting text, moving it around to *organize* the *content* into an inverted pyramid formula to Navigate my reader. If I was missing something in a "who what when where why how or how much" category, all I had to do was make another phone call to generate more *content* to plug into my outline.

Once the *content* was fleshed out and *organized*, I'd clean up the writing, look over the *mechanics*, Punctuate, and then submit it to my editor.

My stories literally started to Right themselves. Gone were the hours of agonizing and painstakingly trying to pull the writing from the depths of my soul before the deadline. The words were right there on the page!

Now that I have a laptop, my notes get typed directly into a document when I'm in class or interviewing a source, eliminating one step in the process and increasing efficiency.

The trick that I learned by accident: don't try to face The Blank Page by staring at it.

Facing a page full of words invites some of that 10:59 a.m. satisfaction to the job early on, and the sooner I was able to relax into the task at hand, the easier the process unfolded.

Getting something—anything—on the page is otherwise known as "prewriting." Freewriting is one of the techniques of prewriting, which is the second step in the writing process.

(Full disclosure: "prewriting" doesn't have to be "freewriting." It can be "mind mapping" or "clustering" or "outlining" or "5WH$." It can be "Voodoo" if that's what works best for you, the keyword being "works best" and if that's the case, I'm going to insist on a full accounting.)

Prewriting can take many shapes at this stage. My method uses "freewriting" because, in the interest of time, I want you to actually meet your application deadline and words on the page are an important step toward this goal.

Cringe if you wish, but trust me on this: do it the way I recommend now and then, once you learn the full process, you have my blessing to experiment with and use any prewriting technique you fancy.

WRITING IS A COMPLICATED ART

Don't tell me the moon is shining; show me the glint of light on broken glass.
—Anton Chekhov

In order to elicit an emotional response from readers, a writer needs to enter the limbic system of the brain, which can only be done through the senses.

Painters, photographers, chefs, dancers, sculptors, musicians—these artists work in materials that are fundamental to the senses. An eater, for example, can immediately taste what the chef creates; a viewer can immediately experience the painter or the photographer; the audience can immediately hear the orchestra or the musician.

The same cannot be said for writers.

Writers craft with words, and words strike the eye first as symbols which then must be translated into the sense that the language signifies and evokes.

Adding to the complexity: readers bring their own memories and experiences to the piece from which they will then begin to decode the meaning of the words—and at that point, it may or may not be the meaning the writer intended.

Eliciting an emotional response from readers by entering the limbic system of the brain, therefore, is the ultimate task of the writer. Since it can only be done through a reader's senses, a writer must *show*, not *tell*.

The task for writers is to connect with readers by stringing words together to exchange information or news or ideas, to COMMUNICATE the exchange of information, news, or ideas.

Unlike creative writing or news reporting or simply sending business emails, academic writing's general purpose is to fulfill a requirement for assessment. Academic writing requires a student to approach a topic with an open mind, research with curiosity, think critically about findings, and clearly convey an understanding of complex concepts and ideas in a structured essay in order to demonstrate learning.

For this reason, academic writing is mainly presented in the third person with a formal style that reflects a logical pattern of reasoning for the main argument (or thesis) of the text.

Therefore, two additional components are necessary for communication to be successful: the first of those is organization.

INTRODUCTION	tell me what you're going to tell me	GENERATE INTEREST	
SUPPORTING IDEA 1	tell me	CREDIBILITY	chronological
SUPPORTING IDEA 2	tell me	LOGIC	spatial
SUPPORTING IDEA 3	tell me	APPEAL	order of importance
CONCLUSION	tell me what you just told me	CHALLENGE READER	
POLISHED MECHANICS THROUGHOUT: GRAMMAR, PUNCTUATION, SPELLING			

The conventional five-point "hamburger" we all loved to hate in high school might be boring or predictable for a college essay, but it's effective; it brings unification and organization to a body of writing that most academics identify with. The persuasive rhetorical mode allows a student to establish a common familiarity with an instructor, especially needed if the instructor isn't familiar with the student's work.

Pay attention. Start to notice the patterns of organization in the writing around you. Observe the predictability.

A business email, for example, typically begins with a salutation, greeting, and pleasantries to open and close the discussion. The center portion then positively affirms the relationship or connection, then addresses the problem, concern, or need, then suggests in a positive way possible solutions for both parties.

If a business email were colors, it would look something like this:

This organization within bodies of writing helps NAVIGATE a reader; this helps to facilitate the communication. Without this guidance, the writing risks meandering off the page, with the reader's attention soon to follow.

Finally, the last component of successful writing is mechanics, which is the usual dread of grammar, punctuation, and spelling. It's not sexy per se, but it's the attention to polishing and details that make the overall work more appealing. Students should use language that is easily understood and conveys the exact meaning of their ideas and thoughts that is supported by empirical evidence from reliable academic sources. Whereas content and organization separate the amateurs from the pros, word choice and mechanics often separate the As from the Cs. To PUNCTUATE means to polish the mechanics of grammar, spelling, *and* punctuation.

When following the Steps in the Righting Process and the 80/20 Rule of Righting, the writing process is entirely demystified. Students no longer waste valuable time staring at the blank page and instead get right to work. The clarity of thought illustrated by formulas and practice significantly reduces the stress and anxiety many students feel when approaching essay assignments.

It is essential that students develop the proper tone, technique, and style for written assignments. Developing good academic writing skills has many advantages beyond obtaining higher grades.

Once a student has improved his or her academic writing skills, the ability to think critically and naturally in a logical and objective manner becomes muscle memory. The student's communication skills will improve remarkably and this will benefit students long after graduation as professionals in their field of expertise.

MISTAKES NO. 6–11

Talking about a passion

Puhleeeeeze don't tell me that you have a "passion" for [insert whatever here.]
    In fact, please don't use the word "passion" in your college application essay. Period.
    Instead, *show me* what that passion led you to *do*.

Telling someone else's story

If you have a friend who got into a tight spot or a family member with a medical struggle, that's their story, not yours. If you sat back on the sidelines, paralyzed with fear or worry, that's understandable—but it's still their story.

If you volunteered to help others who suffer in the same ways as your loved ones, then you're an active participant in the story. If you spent time and energy giving comfort, caregiving, working toward a solution, or helping in some way, then it's your story.

The college application essay begins and ends with you. Make sure your story is yours by confirming your active involvement in the narrative.

Telling the wrong story

Do you want to be remembered as the applicant who wrote about *that*? No.

Make sure that your story keeps you in mind in a positive light, not in an uncomfortable, controversial, or condescending way. Your readers have filters that may be quite different from yours. Your story is about you, not your reader, but you want to be able to communicate with your reader no matter who your reader is.

Forcing a repurposed essay

It's tempting. It's understandable. There are a *lot* of essays in this process. Admissions officers understand this.

It's often possible to repurpose an essay, but it almost always requires the tweaking of at least one or two lines to address specifically the question posed by the prompt. Attention to detail is needed in this direction, do not overlook this!

Forcing a fairy-tale ending

Some things in life can't be fixed.

And sometimes, the stories that we tell haven't quite ended. You might be midway through an experience or midway to reaching a goal. Forcing a happy ending of words is often feels uncomfortable for the reader.

Feeling all the feels

I don't mean to sound cruel when I tell you that I don't care what you think, feel, want, hope for, or believe. But it's true. I don't want to hear it.

What I *do* want to hear is what those thoughts, feelings, wants, hopes, and beliefs *made you do*.

Talk is cheap. Actions speak louder than words. If you can't tell me a story that illustrates your thoughts, beliefs, hopes, and dreams, then hurry up and get out there to create one! Chop chop.

THE TWELFTH MOST COMMON MISTAKE STUDENTS MAKE

It's not an autobiography.

It's a story. Your story.

We like to say the college application essay begins and ends with *you*. What we mean by that is twofold:

1. Expect to use the first-person narrative in this essay. The first-person narrative is a storytelling rhetorical mode in which the storyteller recounts events from their own point of view using the first person such as "I." You are the protagonist in your college application essay.

Having said that, just because it happened to you doesn't make it interesting. We're going to talk more about this later. For now, let's focus on the fundamental lesson of what makes a first-person narrative interesting, which brings us to our second point:

2. Remember your audience.

Your audience is admissions officers, and your audience is expecting *you* to communicate a story (narrative) from your perspective (first person) that gives them an idea of who you are and what you are all about. Your audience is imagining you in their campus environment, wondering what skills, leadership, or academic strengths you will bring to the campus, but also what you may take advantage of while you are there to grow and expand as a student.

Your grades and test scores are going to tell the story of whether or not admissions officers can reasonably expect you to thrive academically, eventually matriculate, and become an alumni donor.

Your college application essay will tell them a completely different story—*your* story. It will tell admissions officers the story of who you are outside of class.

The twelfth biggest mistake students make is either listing their résumé bullets or telling their entire life story.

Imagine reading my résumé.

How fascinated are you by the third line?

This is not your autobiography. This essay is *not* a complete list of your life and times.

Think of your college application essay as more of a short story. It's a snippet. It's a sliver of life that you're sharing with them that gives them just a glimpse of who *you* are. Just a sliver. One experience.

For some of you, this will sound easy! For others, it will sound hard.

It's both. It's a tremendous relief to only have to write a six-hundred-word essay rather than a sixty-thousand-word autobiography. On the flip side, it's terrifying to choose only one snippet of your life experience to define and explain the essence of who you are.

There are a few other considerations as well. Readers may have very different backgrounds, experiences, and filters from yours. So within those six hundred words, you have to write in a way that regardless of those filters, you will be understood.

You have to avoid putting words into your reader's mouths or speaking for them because when you do that, at best, you risk alienation; at worst, you risk offending the reader or coming across as condescending.

This is what I want you to imagine admissions officers seeing when they open your essay:

I believe you are a *great* student who has a *fantastic* story to tell, and I love nothing more than to help you do that. I'm going to hand you the formula and we're going to work through it together.

A NOTE ON INTRODUCTIONS AND CONCLUSIONS

    The name Elizabeth is four syllables and, consequently, has over 20 nicknames. Often, when I introduce myself to others, one of the first questions people ask me is, "Do you have a nickname?" The truth is, I have many nicknames. It seems that my family invents new nicknames for me everyday, ranging from Libby to L3 (Little Libby Loo, a nickname from when I was six) to Tweetie Bird (so named for my childhood love of the cartoon character). The list goes on. For a while, I was even called "Cookie" for my deep and unabated love of freshly-baked chocolate chip cookies and all things chocolate (although the nickname didn't quite stick, this, however, has not gone away, and I have been known to even combine cookie/brownie mixes when baking). Despite my abundance of nicknames, however, I go by Elizabeth.
    Although these nicknames have their origins in relatively superficial things about my life, one nickname my family has given me that sheds the most light into who I am is "Why Girl."

Elizabeth didn't need my help writing an essay. She knocked out a rough draft of her college application essay just fine. She submitted it to me in hopes that I would "edit" it for her.

    I didn't find any dangling participles or noun/verb agreement problems. Not one typo, no punctuation marks missing or out of place.

    Curiously, what I did find was that it took her 477 words to begin answering the question posed in the essay prompt.

    For 477 words, Elizabeth talked about her four-syllable name and the resulting nicknames. In an essay that was 649 of the required 650 words or less.

    Seventy-three percent of her essay was not even focused on answering the question posed in the essay prompt!

    Elizabeth had two sentences in her beautifully written, flawless essay that posed a thoughtful response to the prompt, and they began at word number 478:

    "Learning to ask why again meant discarding my preconceived notions of success. Learning to ask why meant learning to embrace failure as a stepping stone instead of a pitfall."

    Elizabeth wasn't happy with me when I sent her back to the drawing board. Elizabeth can *write*.

RIGHT MY COLLEGE APPLICATION ESSAY

(Her introduction was interesting to read. It probably could easily be published in any number of teen magazines. It just didn't satisfy the requirement for a college application essay.)

Elizabeth needed to Right her college application essay.

*****

The function of the introduction is twofold:

1. To get the reader interested
2. To introduce the topic of the essay

The introduction is an invitation to readers to first consider what you have to say, and then follow your train of thought as you expand upon your thesis statement.

First impressions are crucial, and the introduction can immediately affect the limbic system of your reader's mind, which is why it is so important to your essay. If your introductory paragraph is dull or disjointed, your reader probably will not have much interest in continuing with the essay.

Some standard introduction styles:

- Appealing to their emotions
- Using logic
- Beginning with a provocative question or opinion, one that provokes or stimulates the reader
- Opening with a startling statistic or surprising fact
- Raising a question or series of questions
- Presenting an explanation or rationalization for your essay
- Opening with a relevant quotation or incident
- Opening with a striking, written image
- Including a personal anecdote, or a brief narrative detailing something you have experienced
- General: introduce the thesis and several related points intended for the body of the essay
- Anecdote: begin by telling a brief, true story that relates to the thesis.
- Statistics: begin by quoting startling statistics or surprising facts related to the thesis
- Current Events: begin by referring to well-known recent events that relate to the thesis
- Quote: begin with a famous or compelling quote that relates to the thesis
- "What if?" begins by having the reader imagine a situation that relates to the thesis

Likewise, the function of the conclusion is twofold:

1. To signal the end of the essay
2. To wrap up the various points of the essay

A conclusion wraps up the essay in a clear and interesting way and includes the reasoning behind the judgment or decision reached by the writer (otherwise known as a thesis) as a result of the synthesis of the material. While there may be some reiteration of previous points, it does not simply list or repeat (summarize) what has already been written.

To achieve a sense of unity, a strong conclusion brings the reader back to some element of the introduction when wrapping up the essay. For example, if the intro begins with an anecdote, refer back to it in the conclusion.

Instead of starting and ending at rough draft with her next essay, Elizabeth used the steps in the writing process. She listened to my instruction. She used The 80/20 Rule of RIGHTING and fleshed out her content, rhetorical mode, and organizational method long before she began to worry about mechanics.

Elizabeth copied and pasted the essay prompt to keep it top-of-mind on the page:

> Describe a topic, idea, or concept you find so engaging that it makes you lose all track of time. Why does it captivate you? What or who do you turn to when you want to learn more?

In 643 words, she *showed* Georgia Tech her answer, sandwiched between her introduction and conclusion:

> (Introduction) My elbows rest uncomfortably on the metal patio table, red chile chicken enchiladas on a plate in front of me. I stare at the board: my rook and queen are targeted at the dark-square bishop, defended by the queen and rook. I could almost pull a backrank checkmate, if not for the queen. Rook takes, bishop takes, queen takes, queen takes. No...what about interrupting the line of defense? Making a sacrifice to force the queen to move? I go with this and play out the sequence.
>
> "Checkmate," I declare. A look of pride comes across Baba's face; he chuckles, and we shake hands. "Good game."
>
> This was one of the first games I ever won against Baba, my chess teacher since age six. At the time we played this game, I was in a middle school phase dominated by power-chain braces, clothes that didn't quite fit, and a sudden affinity for Green Day, and I had recently become interested in learning chess strategy. Baba gave me lessons on the patio that day, which served as my launchpad to begin seeking out information on my own.
>
> Nowadays, I play chess online nearly every day, solving tactics puzzles, playing games, reading up on strategy, and watching live streams. I never expected to get anything out of chess except enjoyment, but looking back, chess has played a big role in helping me understand my interests and where I'm going.

My story begins with a blue and red book currently sitting on the fifth shelf of my bookcase called *What Color Is Your Parachute? (for teens)*. My aunt gifted me this book the July before tenth grade, a time I remember being confused about where I was going, what I enjoyed, and what I wanted out of my future. One of the book's questions was, "What's something you do simply because you love it?" I made a list, and, near the top, was chess. Why do I like chess? I decided it certainly wasn't because of the tournaments or a desire to get a higher ranking. On the piece of paper, next to the word chess, I had written the word "puzzles." I realized I enjoy the thinking process that goes into chess, the kind that's used to solve a puzzle. Seeing and calculating moves, piecing together positions and little advantages—this I find exciting. That July, I determined that, no matter what my specific career is in the future, I would like to be solving a problem, putting together pieces of a puzzle. This was a major stepping stone for me.

Fast forward to my eleventh-grade physics class. Physics, I discovered that year, was like chess in that it has tiny bits of information that, when pieced together, paint a larger picture or give insight into a certain clue. What I find so compelling about physics is that, unlike in chess, where the object of the game is to gain an advantage over the opposite side, in physics, the implications are enormous: from colonizing Mars to piloting a rocket, to sending a car to space with the Hitchhiker reference "Don't Panic." Sometimes the implications are small: when I'm driving on the highway and thinking about torque on my wheels and frictional force, angular acceleration, and equilibrium. It's because of my interest in physics and space that I want to major in aerospace engineering.

(Conclusion) Discovering my true interests was a long and winding path that, for me, began with a checkered 8×8 board.

She got in.

Pro tip: There's a difference between a summary and a conclusion. A summary quite literally sums up the points made in an essay. It reiterates what the reader can expect to glean from reading. It's a regurgitation of content. For this reason, a summary is generally considered a boring and ineffective way to end a paper.

STUDENT ESSAY: SHORT ANSWER

Virginia Tech Essay Prompts (Strongly Recommended):

You may respond to up to three of the essay prompts below (choose one, two, or three) as you feel they support your individual application. In general, concise, straightforward writing is often the best for college essays. Please limit your responses to no more than three hundred words in length.

Tell a story from your life, describing an experience that either demonstrates your character or helped to shape it. (300 words)

    I was born in Tokyo. I've lived in two countries and five states. Four times in my life, I've had to be "The New Kid," starting over in new neighborhoods, new schools, and meeting new friends. It wasn't easy, but I had no choice; my father's Air Force career transplanted us to the West, Midwest, East Coast, and now South. My first day of high school, I was without the safety net of elementary school friends. I stood looking out into a sea of unfamiliar kids and silently started to panic. Mrs. Macaluso caught my eye and quickly rescued me. She welcomed me, and then led me to a table, introduced me to the guys sitting there, and basically gave me an "in" to start that first day. Last summer, I found myself in the same figurative place, surrounded by strangers at the beginning of the weeklong programs I attended on college campuses. I thought about how I'd described to the kid who became my best friend in high school what it was like to move around so much: the Air Force would take me away from my friends and put me in front of strangers—but those strangers always turn out to be my friends; I just hadn't met them yet. Next fall, as I begin college, I'm actually excited about being surrounded by all of the friends I have yet to meet. (234 words)

Why Virginia Tech (300 words)

    Virginia Tech was the first college I toured. The night before, my mom, sister, and I got three hours of sleep in between flying to Baltimore and driving to Blacksburg for an early morning tour. I was tired, groggy, and unsure of what to expect. All of my reasons for wanting to attend Virginia Tech were revealed to me that morning on the tour:

1. I always thought a "Hokie" was a turkey, but learned it's in fact an invented cheer, and burnt orange and Chicago maroon were chosen to give the school a unique appearance. These quirky aspects just scream fun.
2. I want a college that will challenge me intellectually, but also offer a fun escape from the grind of schoolwork.
3. Ut Prosim: VT students give back to the community of Blacksburg through student-organized service. This is the sense of community and camaraderie I'm looking to become a part of.
4. I loved living in Virginia, and want to move back.
5. The food. (Seriously. The food.) (166 words)

STUDENT ESSAY: SHORT ANSWER

(Prompt) In the MIT application, we're not looking for one long, highly-polished essay. Instead, interspersed throughout the application will be short answer questions designed to help us get to know you. Just be yourself.

At MIT, we bring people together to better the lives of others. MIT students work to improve their communities in different ways, from tackling the world's biggest challenges to being a good friend. Describe one way in which you have contributed to your community, whether in your family, the classroom, your neighborhood, etc. (*) (200–250 words)

I wish you could feel how unbelievably hot that August Louisiana day was. One kid passed out. My high school gave seniors the day off, but arranged for a bus to take volunteers to Baton Rouge to assist in flood recovery. I thought about the newspaper images, the "Cajun Navy" zipping through the streets in boats filled with overwhelmed people. Houses were submerged to the rooftops. I had no idea how people were going to make sense of such a wreck. Curious, I went. We joined Habitat for Humanity at one house and carried out all of the appliances, drove sledgehammers through walls, peeled away the drywall, tore out the damaged wood underneath, and carried out belongings that could still be salvaged (like silverware). Our goggles fogged up and we couldn't see anything, so we took them off and stuff fell in our eyes. Our masks got sweaty, so we took those off too, and the stench of rotten and wet was intolerable. It seemed "rebuilding" needed to begin with everything being completely torn apart. What fueled us to keep moving through the humidity and seemingly insurmountable work is exactly what made all the difference in our contribution: community. We were strength in numbers, people showing up because others needed our help and doing in numbers what would have taken someone forever to do all alone. We got to work, and one-by-one checked off entire tasks so that a house could once again promise hope, family, and future. (248 words)

STUDENT ESSAY: SHOW ME, DON'T TELL ME

Tell a story from your life, describing an experience that either demonstrates your character or helped to shape it. (600 words)

I remember blinding white when I could finally pry open my eyes.

The soft, high-pitched beeping of pulse monitors, the whir of an oxygen mask machine, and the sound of my rattling breath filled the still room. I winced as I moved my swollen arms under the starchy white sheets.

"You can't keep doing this," my mom said sadly. "I know you love them, but we can't keep coming to the hospital every time you see a cat."

I tried to open my mouth to protest, but my lips were too swollen to talk properly. This was not the first time this had happened. My parents tried to keep me away from animals because they knew how disastrous it would be, but nothing could stop me from weaseling my way through their preventative tactics. I love animals, and nothing would stop me from getting to be around them.

Since then, I have recovered from my severe allergies because of allergy shots, but I will never forget those days.

I first heard about veterinarians when I was a child in elementary school. In the fifth-grade classroom one day, there was an extensive setup for career day where parents come in and do a sort of "show-and-tell" about their jobs, and the teacher explains other careers. In my mind, adulthood was so far away and so complicated that I didn't pay much attention to career day, but I did notice that a majority of the girls picked veterinarian as their first choice. They sat in clusters around the room, gushing about how much they loved animals and how cute animals were. I didn't want to be a follower, so I picked something else.

As the years went on, I noticed something about that kind of people and about myself. While I was excited to see and love animals no matter what, other people had very conditional love. They did not love sick animals. They did not love "ugly" animals. They did not love old animals, or smelly animals, or any animal that wasn't "cute." No one shared my excitement when I saw dirty stray dogs or cats or dogs that were so old, they couldn't even walk to the back door.

It hurt my heart because I knew those animals need love too. I told them so all the time.

Recently, I got my own dog, and although she is fluffy, clean, and healthy, I love her unconditionally. I love her spirit, her personality, her (almost) constant happiness, and even the little moods she gets into when we eat pizza for dinner and don't share. I believe that she is just as complicated and just as intelligent as we are, and she deserves the same quality health care as any human being.

Last summer, I went to camp, and while everyone else was splashing in the pool, I was picking ticks off of the smelly, stray dogs in the area and getting them clean water. I am completely dedicated to helping and loving animals because I understand that not all people have the same passion as I do, or the same ability to look past dirt or sickness. I strive to make animals the healthiest and happiest they can be so that their owners can spend joyful, quality time with their pets.

I aim to attend and finish veterinarian school to follow my dream because in recent years, I have realized the rarity of my depth of care for animals, especially the sick ones. (585 words)

STUDENT ESSAY: LESSONS FROM FAILURE

Prompt: The lessons we take from failure can be fundamental to later success. Recount an incident or time when you experienced failure. How did it affect you, and what did you learn from the experience? (500–700 words)

In fifth grade, my parents signed me up for swim team. I hated it. There was no ball, no strategy, just endless laps and stroke mechanics.

We generally weren't allowed to quit an activity mid-season, but after much negotiation, my parents finally agreed to let me swap swimming for learning to play the saxophone.

Fast forward six years, and my boss at the pool where I'm a lifeguard informed me that the board of directors made a new policy that all lifeguards would be automatically signed up for the club's swim team, and my first meet would be next weekend.

So there I was, in my lifeguard shorts, standing on the starting block for the 100-meter freestyle, just a few lanes over from one of the star swimmers from my high school's swim team. No pressure.

Look, I can swim. Lifeguards are trained in endurance swimming, long distances, long stretches of floating, and treading water.

Swim team swimmers, on the other hand, train fast-twitch muscles to swim *fast*.

Lifeguards don't dive into the pool, we jump—we're trained not to take our eyes off of a struggling swimmer.

Swim team swimmers perfect their dives in order to streamline their entry into the water, and they glide underwater for as long as possible to maximize speed.

Swim team swimmers have elegant flip turns at the edges of the pool. Lifeguards have awkward, unpracticed flip-turns and aim only to reach the edge of the pool once, the oasis for saving lives.

Standing on the block with these realizations, swimming the 100-meter freestyle felt like the worst thing that could possibly happen to me. I felt the weight of my own ineptitude as I measured myself against a classmate who trained hard year-round for this very moment.

And it didn't get any better in the water. I couldn't breathe, my muscles ached, and my head kept reminding me that I'd be last place—if I finished at all.

Yes, the worst happened: I came in last.

I climbed from the pool and retreated, fearing I was a big disappointment to my team.

I learned three very important life lessons:

First, the most formidable opponent I have is my own ego. As it turned out since not all of the teams had a male swimmer in my age group, the fact that I at least finished ended up earning us some points.

Second, I learned to watch more carefully as a lifeguard presiding over swim meets (whereas before, I thought I was a formality.)

Third, I learned that the worst that can happen is never the worst that can happen.

In the fall of our senior year, alumnus Harold Bologna wobbled a bit on his prosthetic legs toward the front of our class, barely a year after the explosion. He told us how what seemed like the worst thing that could happen to him—when he learned from the nurse that his legs were gone after he stepped on an explosive device during a combat mission—turned out to be an opportunity that he never would have discovered.

First, though, he had to get up and relearn how to walk.

Harold's a Navy SEAL, and that's what those guys do—they get up and learn to walk even after they find out their legs have been blown off.

So there's a guy at my high school who can beat me in the 100-meter freestyle.

There's also a guy from my high school who really did face the worst thing that could happen to him on that day, and yet he went on to overcome it.

Harold put a face and a purpose on a spark that had been ignited in me for some time, solidifying my interest in biomedical engineering. I didn't put two and two together until I sat down to write this essay, but the Harolds of this world are living, breathing examples of why I want to major in biomedical engineering and possibly continue on to medical school.

Giving people hope that the worst that can happen is never the worst that can happen is just the beginning of what I learned from swimming that 100-meter freestyle. (696 words)

STUDENT ESSAY: SIGNIFICANT EXPERIENCE

PROMPT: The University of Oregon is interested in hearing more about you. Write an essay of 500 words or less that shares information that we cannot find elsewhere on your application. Any topic you choose is welcome. Some ideas you might consider include your future ambitions and goals, a special talent, extracurricular activity, or unusual interest that sets you apart from your peers, or a significant experience that influenced your life.

"Cowgirl up," Gramps says, with a sprinkle of challenge in his tone.

That was one of the first phrases I learned. There are four of us, all girls, born into our grandpa's ranch life, and Gramps used that phrase to insist we could do anything.

There was always work to be done on the ranch, from putting up fences to branding cattle to calving and lambing. Something was always broken or needed work, and that's where us grandkids came in handy. Gramps always had jobs for us to do, and there was no telling how long they were going to take. We couldn't go inside until the job was done, and there was no cheating in the process. Only the best work was given approval and counted as a job well done. There was never an easy way out, and "no" or "I can't" was never a choice.

The problem started when we grew old enough to ride horses to gather or move cows. This was something I never wanted to do. Riding horses was something I had a big fear of and was not confident doing. Having to control that large animal and not knowing if it was going to go my way was very frightening. I just wanted the horse to listen to me, but that doesn't always happen. For everyone else in my family, it came naturally.

I stopped helping, but not being part of the job meant not being part of the family activities. I felt like I was missing out on the fun with my sister and cousins and disappointing Gramps.

Gramps wasn't mad that I didn't feel comfortable riding horses. He just expected me to "cowgirl up," to find some other way to contribute.

So that's what I did. I learned how to ride the four-wheeler. I rode in front of the pack while calling the cattle that came bolting behind me. I wasn't sure how to accomplish this task at first but in the end, I was able to prove to myself that fear wasn't going to hold me back and my urge to problem-solve ended up being pretty fun. On my four-wheeler, I "cowgirl upped" and got the job done.

Gramps inspired me to set my fears aside and persevere. It didn't matter whether I was male or female, young or old, what mattered was the lesson: I can do it. Being on Gramp's ranch, working difficult jobs, and overcoming challenges tested every part of me. Those challenges taught me that what's important to me, such as hard work, problem-solving, and doing everything to your best ability the first time.

In the end, I know how to "cowgirl up" and get the job done. (452 words)

STUDENT ESSAY: UNUSUAL WAY TO HAVE FUN

PROMPT: Caltech students have long been known for their quirky sense of humor, whether it be through planning creative pranks, building elaborate party sets, or even the year-long preparation that goes into our annual Ditch Day. Please describe an unusual way in which you have fun. (200 words max)

    It's not my regular group of friends, and the only thing predictable about the game is that today will be completely different from any other. Fifteen guys from my senior class have a group text meetup for gaming. When any combination of us meets up inside a game, we don't follow the rules. In fact, we try to be absurd as possible, setting unrealistic challenges and goals and creating ridiculous restrictions that lead to sub-games. One example of a game-within-a-game that we play is "line patrol" where one player does everything he can to stop the others from crossing a randomly placed line. We award one another points for imagination and creativity when defining the sub-game rules. One of my favorite aspects of playing familiar games with these offbeat rules is that I interact with people I'd otherwise not normally hang out with at school. Guys from all different walks of our senior class come together to play—athletes, honor students, and every other group in between. Our gaming community is almost like a world of its own. (178 words)

STUDENT ESSAY: RESEARCH

PROMPT: Other parts of your application give us a sense for how you might contribute to Northwestern. But we also want to consider how Northwestern will contribute to your interests and goals. In 300 words or less, help us understand what aspects of Northwestern appeal most to you, and how you'll make use of specific resources and opportunities here.

When I arrived at Northwestern earlier this fall for a visit, I really didn't expect much. I'd been on a lot of college tours and have seen a lot of manicured grounds with great lecture halls and enticing cities in their backyards. As I walked along the campus tour, Northwestern distinguished itself from other tours by standing out. I was impressed by the possibility I saw in almost everything that was pointed out and explained. I could imagine myself, like our tour guide from Atlanta, making friends with fellow students who come from all over the world, painting and guarding the fountain/rock, and finding my way around engineering as a major. (He shared how he was able to narrow his focus from his experiences both in class and on campus.) After listening to the first-year engineering curriculum and the advice for incoming freshmen that McCormick's Assistant Dean, Ms. Worsdall, had to share with us, I was completely blown away by things that I hadn't even realized I needed, things that Northwestern has already identified as a superior, systemic method of educating engineers. The idea that as a first-term freshman, I'll be collaborating with others to help a client from the Rehabilitation Institute of Chicago made me incredibly excited to start school and dive right into my future career! I appreciate the emphasis on communication, as I've worked hard to improve my writing and speaking skills in high school and want to continue improving them. I also liked the reasoning my tour guide gave as to why the quarter system better benefits the students. I'm interested in medical school, and the experiential, right-brain, left-brain curriculum in biomedical engineering is everything I'd hoped for and more in preparing me to achieve my long-term educational goals. (294 words)

STUDENT ESSAY:
RESEARCH | DIVERSITY

Our families and communities often define us and our individual worlds. Community might refer to your cultural group, extended family, religious group, neighborhood or school, sports team or club, co-workers, etc. Describe the world you come from and how you, as a product of it, might add to the diversity of the University of Washington. Maximum length: 300 words

Chairs line the streets days before the parade. It's small-town Americana at its best—classic cars, tractors, bands, politicians shaking hands, and the Little League handing out candy. Literally the whole town participates in the tradition. Afterward, we move toward the Columbia River to wait for the magic. The crowd quiets as the first light shoots up and BOOM, the fireworks burst, colors reflecting off the calm river.

The annual Ridgefield Fourth of July celebration was the highlight of my childhood summers.

As I grew up and branched out, I became part of something bigger than myself—community. Volunteering at the Community Resource Center, I built a strong relationship with a fifth grader. Sophia always wanted to play Uno, even when the other kids did not. I played hours on end with Sophia, who showed me how much little things can mean to others. For three years as an outdoor school counselor, I led the next generation of students in my community. The first day was the toughest: the kids didn't listen and wanted to go home. I told them ghost stories, played cards, and talked to them about girls (you know, typical boy stuff). By week's end, they listened respectfully and did not want to leave. Over the years, during the annual food drive, I observed elderly and lower-income homes donating at our local food bank, showing me that people are generous despite their limitations.

Community is much more than annual celebrations or personal achievements—it's about being an active participant, engaging deeply, and giving back. What I bring to the Husky community is deep engagement with those who fill the chairs around me, forming a community that is bigger than any of us as individuals. (287 words)

CHRISTINE GACHARNÁ

JUMPSTARTS

EXPLORE TOPICS, IDEAS & POSSIBLE EXPERIENCES

If you don't yet have an experience that you feel confident in writing about, there's still time — get out there and find one!

Working a summer or part-time job where an indicent you faced presented a dilemma

Witnessing the unfairness or mistreatment of another individual

Volunteering to help a neighborhood recover after a natural disaster

Pushing yourself athletically to an achievement you are proud of

Experiencing a physical limitation, challenge, or difference

Devising a creative solution to a problem when you didn't like the alternatives presented

Learning a new skill that empowers you to do something you were unable to do before

Helping a friend through a situation neither of you had prior experience navigating

Lending a hand to someone in need and realizing you benefitted more than they did

Facing a situation where you were powerless to change the outcome yet learned from it

Standing up to an idea or experience that violates your personal code of ethics

Supporting an idea, cause, or political campaign and learning someting new in the process

Learning a surprising life lesson you weren't expecting via another person, pet, or experience

Creating a project or a piece of art that garnered praise and/or admiration from your community

"Regardless of how anyone treats you, you stand to benefit. While some people teach you who you do want to be, others teach you who you don't want to be. And it's the people who teach you who you don't want to be that provide some of the most lasting and memorable lessons on social graces, human dignity, and the importance of acting with integrity." —KARI KAMPAKIS

RIGHT MY COLLEGE APPLICATION ESSAY

NARRATION + CHRONOLOGICAL

STORYTIME ALL OF A SUDDEN,
SET STORY PRIOR TO,
SHOW STORY MEANWHILE,
CLIMAX IN THAT INSTANT,
SHOW CHANGE AT THE SAME TIME,
FINAL SCENE SINCE
MORAL OF STORY THESE DAYS,

[PASTE PROMPT HERE]

Jump right into telling your story.

Wait, back up, identify who, where, when, set the scene so the reader understands where they are. Remember, you're the navigator and they're there with you, so you need to lead.

Chronologically lead the reader right up to the very moment when everything changes.

SHOW the moment when everything changes. (Show me, don't tell me.)

Begin the conclusion by SHOWING chronological events that happened as a result of that moment.

SHOW the final scene that directly relates to the significance of the story & prompt.

SHOW the significance, value, importance, and/or relevance of coming to terms with this resulting change. Remember: if there has been no significant change, there is no college application essay.

INDEX

A
Academic writing 3, 17, 18, 66, 100, 101, 103
ACT 24, 43

C
Chronological organizational method 64, 72, 75, 77, 78, 127
Communicate 7, 9, 17, 18, 21, 46, 54, 60, 66, 67, 107, 108
Conclusion 53, 57, 72, 81, 82, 110, 112, 113

E
Editing 11, 26, 66, 78, 79, 85, 92, 98, 100
ESL 23

F
Final draft 90
Five-point hamburger essay 22, 54, 62, 104
Freewriting 3, 5, 7, 8, 17, 23, 41, 42, 45, 57, 58, 65, 75, 76, 77, 101, 102

I
Introduction 53, 72, 74, 110, 111, 112

M
Mental models 14, 15, 23
Mistakes, most common 25, 42

N
Narrative rhetorical mode 58, 62, 63, 65, 74, 127
Navigate 6, 17, 19, 21, 49, 79
Noncognitive variables 13, 24, 27, 28, 29, 49, 77

O
Organizational methods 21, 53, 62, 63, 66, 101
Outline 23, 41, 45, 60, 70, 72, 73, 74, 75, 76, 77, 102

P
Persuasive rhetorical mode 53, 56, 62, 64, 72, 104
Prewriting 4, 6, 23, 25, 45, 58, 101, 102
Punctuate 17, 19, 79

R
Research 28, 56, 57, 66, 67, 68, 69, 73, 75, 77, 103, 124, 125
Revising 11, 78, 79, 81, 100
Rhetorical modes xix, 21, 53, 61, 63, 66, 101
Rough draft 3, 6, 11, 20, 22, 23, 25, 42, 46, 47, 48, 57, 58, 66, 71, 73, 76, 77, 78, 110, 112

S
Sample student essay 45
SAT 43
Show me, dont tell me 56, 75, 86, 117

T
The 80/20 Rule of RIGHTING 16, 20, 26, 27, 56, 66, 73, 105, 112
The Blank Page 4, 23, 66, 73, 97, 99, 100, 102, 105
The Five Whys 7
The Resistance 6, 15, 42
The Steps in the RIGHTING Process 9, 18, 19, 20, 22, 27, 45, 49, 66, 105

W
Word count 27, 39, 75, 87, 90, 91

ABOUT THE AUTHOR

Back when reading news on paper was still a thing, Christine Gacharná was the editor-in-chief of her campus newspaper and founder of the *Arizona Daily Wildcat* online. She is an award-winning writer and photographer whose work has appeared in numerous newspapers and magazines nationwide as both a staff member and a freelancer. She holds a BA in English from Oregon State University and an MA in journalism from the University of Arizona and is a certified professional photographer.

For six years, she taught college essay writing to undergraduates at the University of Phoenix (Baton Rouge and New Orleans campuses) and, as lead faculty for communication, spearheaded campus policy and efforts to streamline the evaluation and assessment of student writing.

She is the founder and principal editor at Essay Cure, as well as a member in good standing of the Professional Photographers of America, the Society of Professional Journalists, and the Loudoun County (VA) Chamber of Commerce. She lives in Northern Virginia with her husband, Carlos, and their puppy, Aspen.

Printed in the USA
CPSIA information can be obtained
at www.ICGtesting.com
LVHW071524020824
787195LV00044B/772